Writing from the Senses

Writing from the Senses

59 Exercises to Ignite Creativity and Revitalize Your Writing

Laura Deutsch

SHAMBHALA · *Boston & London* · 2014

Shambhala Publications, Inc.
Horticultural Hall
300 Massachusetts Avenue
Boston, Massachusetts 02115
www.shambhala.com

9 8 7 6 5 4 3 2

Printed in the United States of America

Designed by Lora Zorian

♾ This edition is printed on acid-free paper that meets the American National Standards Institute z39.48 Standard.
♻ This book is printed on 30% postconsumer recycled paper.
For more information please visit www.shambhala.com.
Distributed in the United States by Penguin Random House LLC
and in Canada by Random House of Canada Ltd

LIBRARY OF CONGRESS CATALOGING-IN-PUBLICATION DATA

Deutsch, Laura.
Writing from the senses: 59 exercises to ignite creativity
and revitalize your writing / Laura Deutsch.—First edition.
      pages   cm
ISBN 978-1-61180-044-9 (pbk.: acid-free paper)
1. Authorship. I. Title.
PN145.N49 2014
808.02—dc23
2013006695

For my students, whose writing inspires me every day.

Contents

Acknowledgments

I AM SO GRATEFUL to family and friends who read my manuscript with care, providing encouragement, support, and valuable feedback. Special thanks go to my erudite, world-traveling brother, Daniel Deutsch, who polished my Italian and gave me excellent ideas for the section on sound. To my sister, Margery Deutsch—she is my perfect reader and offered great suggestions throughout the book. And with gratitude, to my trusted writing-editing-teaching buddy, Leslie Keenan. I feel fortunate to have you all in my circle.

I thank Susan Hall for her wonderful artwork at the beginning of each section, which adds so much to the book.

Thanks also to those who contributed to *Writing from the Senses*, knowingly or not. Allison Post and Jeri Metz shared expertise on subjects as varied as breathing and gardening. Edward Espe Brown taught me about cooking and meditation. Erica Kaplan read the entire manuscript just for fun. And love and thanks to my parents, Edith and Enoch Deutsch, for the rich life they gave me and for all the great writing material that has come out of the experience.

Deepest thanks to friends and students who generously contributed their writing to this book: Laura Bachman, Debra Baker, Kathy Barr, Valorie Beer, Rita Bral, Gina Catena, Margery Deutsch, Sandra Gatten, Rachael Grossman, Susan Hall, Georgia Hesse, Jeanee Hoffman, Brian Johns, Sheila-Merle

Johnson, Carolyn Kellogg, Laurie McAndish King, Erin Kinikin, Karen Leland, Jessica Levine, Gale Lipsyte, Rachel McClelland, Julia McNeal, Anne Milner, Cynthia Miller Moore, Patricia Morgan, Sandhya Nankani, Basya Petnick, Miriam Phillips, Susan Richard, Jane Rollins, Adrienne Sciutto, Elizabeth Shreeve, Marilyn Steele, Anne-Christine Strugnell, Laurie Szujewska, Wendy Thieler, Catherine Toldi, Mary Van Voorhees, Eli Weiner, Janice Westerling, and Laurel Wilson.

Introduction

A WHIFF OF A CLOVE cigarette catapults me back to a restaurant shack in Indonesia, suspended over the water on rickety wooden stilts.

The sound of a song from the sixties elicits memories of my first teen kiss.

A basket of cooking utensils evokes a student's long-forgotten story of learning how to cook as a child in postwar Belgium.

Our material surrounds us, through memory, imagination, and sensory experiences. From the South of France to the south of India, I have kept notes and written stories. The sights, sounds, tastes, scents, and textures provided material, whether I was describing, musing, imagining, or writing a memory evoked by my surroundings. While it may seem easier to write about exotic places, I've discovered I need not travel halfway around the world to find subjects that inspire my writing.

Writing from the Senses will show you how to tap into an endless source of engaging material, using your senses to develop imagery and details that bring writing alive. With practice you'll recognize the prompts that your daily life provides and use them to trigger your individual stories, from memoir and fiction to travel writing and poetry. Beyond craft, this book can enhance your experience in a wide range of writing, from journaling and journalism to meditative and therapeutic writing.

The techniques I describe and the exercises at the end of each chapter work so well that many students in my workshops have polished the pieces that resulted from these exercises and had them published in magazines, newspapers, books, and online. But while parts of *Writing from the Senses* discuss how to hone your work, this book is not focused on performance or the creation of a product. It is about being present and trusting the creative process.

Before I figured this out, my writing practice was much like my typical yoga workout. I'd pull a chair up to the TV and sip a cup of Peet's Coffee Garuda Blend while I watched Lilias do a half-spinal twist on PBS's *Lilias, Yoga and You*. She'd stretch. I'd sip. Eventually, I got out of my chair and began a consistent yoga practice. My flexibility, strength, and balance improved—as did my attitude and sense of well-being.

And so it is with writing. Writers write. We don't just think about writing, dream, meditate, read, talk, or watch television programs about it. We put pen to paper, fingertips to keyboard. Once I began a consistent writing practice, my sense of well-being, writing flexibility, and strength all improved. As with a yoga practice, the writing exercises in this book can help you get out of your head, into your body, and fully express who you are.

"Working out" in this "writers' gym," you can tone and develop the "muscles" for awareness and sensory detail. Soon, even your freewrites may be richly layered without conscious effort; you'll strengthen your ability to "show, not tell." If you decide to go back and edit, you may add more images, similes, and dialogue, choose lively verbs, and develop your characters' quirky behaviors. This book will help you do that, too.

The chapters in this book contain writing by me and my students to illustrate what can come from doing the exercises and using the prompts presented; they demonstrate how using all your senses can deepen your experience and enrich your writing. I am constantly surprised and delighted by the words that flow from people's pens.

There are many ways you can use *Writing from the Senses*. You may read it for the stories, just as I sipped coffee and watched Lilias do yoga, until you're ready to write—though chances are, if you're reading this, you're ready. You can do the exercises in the order in which they're presented or read chapters at random as they draw you, choose an exercise that grabs your writing mind, and jump right in.

If you're using the book as a learning tool, you may want to read it in sequence.

We begin with "sight," the easiest sense for most people to write about, then move through the other senses: sound, smell, taste, and touch. I've included a section on motion, too, because gestures convey character and help us see a scene. As you progress through the book and start to access your material with ease, you may want to craft it into stories, so there's also a section on how to develop and revise your freewrites.

Initially the exercises guide you to notice and describe what's before you. The prompts are concrete and tangible. Many of the examples are scenes or snapshots rather than stories with well-developed plot and characters. But you need not stay with vignettes or description. Just let the writing come out without planning or control.

When you're ready to go deeper, the prompts in this book can take you there. As you will see, what appears to be a simple prompt can open up memories, feelings, and imagination. This is a wonderful way to develop new material, process the past, and dream of the future.

Often readers know a piece is powerful, but they're not sure why. So from time to time I will point out why I like specific words and phrases, as I do in class or working one on one with writers.

Wherever you start, the exercises will help you bring your world to the page. With *Writing from the Senses* as a guide, you need never again find yourself staring at a blank page, computer screen, crumbs on the carpet, or cracks in the ceiling, wondering how to begin.

Most of these exercises can be done anywhere. That is the beauty of it. Wherever you are, your senses are with you. Awake and aware, you bring your writing to life. Now pick up your pen or turn on your computer. As you read this book, don't force. Allow. Let inspiration move through you. Let your creativity bloom.

Getting Started

If you're new to freewriting, it helps to start by committing to write for a short amount of time. In my classes we begin with seven-minute freewrites, letting the words come through our pens without conscious thought. We work up to longer periods (ten, twenty, even thirty minutes or more). If you don't want to watch the clock, set a timer for seven or ten minutes and write using one of the prompts as soon as you push the "start" button. You are always free to write for a longer time, and eventually seven or ten minutes will fly by. The important thing is to decide before you begin how long you're going to write and write for that entire time.

Remember, we're trusting the process. You may have experienced this in meditation: thoughts and emotions arise unbidden, yet you complete the practice for the predetermined time period. In the same way, I encourage you to stay with your writing and complete your session, even if you've decided to write for only ten minutes.

Alternatively, if you're writing on the computer, you can commit to a certain number of words. Begin with a 300-word minimum. You can check "Word Count" under the "Tools" menu to see how many words you've written; if you haven't reached 300, keep writing.

When freewriting, you're the writer, not the editor. So don't cross out or revise as you go. Just keep writing as fast as you can. If you can't think of a word, write a placeholder. You can come back after the freewrite and edit. For example, I'm picturing a particular kind of tree, but I don't recall the name. If I'm writing by hand, I write "tree," circle it, and move on. Later I'll fill in what kind of tree it was. If I'm writing on the computer, I keep going without underlining or bolding, though some people put brackets or ellipses around words they want to fill in later.

If you can't think of anything to say, write what's coming through your mind— "I have nothing to say. I have nothing to say." "I hate this prompt." "I'd rather write about . . ." Then go there!

This isn't about writing on topic. The prompts are not an assignment. These exercises are designed to help you write whatever comes up and put it onto the page.

What if the minute you begin to write, you're on an entirely different topic? No problem. Let the writing write you. Whatever comes through you is perfect. That's what you're supposed to be writing about. You are the vehicle for creativity and inspiration to move through you. There's no wrong way to do this.

Write without worrying about what other people will think. I would always prefer that you tell your truth on paper or computer, even if you choose not to share it with others. The quirks of your mind and heart are what make your writing engaging to us and useful to you. Forget about social niceties. That means don't be concerned with writing about people who are still alive. Just write it—we'll figure out what to do with it later. It also means don't worry about writing something so intimate and personal that you're writing for your eyes only. You have total freedom to write whatever arises. You can put it in a drawer and show it to no one. Guaranteed to be enlightening, whether or not you realize it in the moment.

Using the freewrite techniques, you may find yourself writing lines and having flashes of inspiration that wouldn't have occurred to you if you'd spent three hours in front of a computer, thinking hard about what to write. You may find a perfect phrase that you can pluck out of a freewrite and insert in a piece you're working on. For example, in a piece I wrote about my father's illness, I hadn't described what he looked like when I entered the hospital room. Readers told me they wanted to "see" him. Sometime later, in a freewrite, I came up with a simple description of my father that worked beautifully in a longer piece about him.

Dad grinned when I pushed open the door to his room—the smile I'd inherited, which shows all thirty-two teeth, clear back to the molars. His small brown eyes twinkled behind rimless glasses. Once broad, he seemed smaller cranked up in his hospital bed, wearing pale blue pajama bottoms and a white T-shirt.

One more thing about this kind of writing: often within a freewrite you'll touch on topics worth exploring in future freewrites. In other words, you'll notice subjects that are important or interesting to you. Writing about them may help you sort things out or even create literature. I read over my freewrites, underlining words and phrases that I want to write more about. This way, I build a list for future writing.

In my freewriting time, I shift between the personal list I've developed, topics that pop into my mind throughout the day, and topics other people suggest.

For virtually every piece I write, whether it's an article, book, or business project, I begin with a freewrite. Once I get my thoughts on paper (without worrying how clever or coherent they are), I can see what's worth keeping, what to discard, what's repetitious, what needs to be developed, and how to organize the piece. In other words, I don't do every freewrite with the idea that I will turn it into a product, but for me, every product begins with a freewrite.

A word on whether it's better to write by hand or on the computer. Many people feel there's a heart connection when writing by hand. I, too, feel a difference. Yet, I usually write on my computer because I can write faster and because I can save my freewrites. I have folders for each year called Writing Practice (Year) or Freewrites (Year). I name each freewrite with a title that will remind me what it's about. (I want to be able to find those perfect lines for pieces I'm working on later.) If you write by hand, consider typing your freewrites into your computer, so that you can access them more easily in the future.

All the exercises can be done alone, but some are fun to do with other writers. You can surprise each other with prompts and encourage each other by your presence. I'll let you know in the following chapters if I think working with a partner can enhance a particular exercise.

PART ONE

Sight

I MAGES TELL THE STORY. Images set the scene. A rubber plantation in India, white sap dripping down smooth tree trunks, rows of silent sentries in the shadowed woods. A childhood bedroom with quilted red corduroy bedspreads, wallpaper patterned with pink and red carnations. A father's white Ford Fairlane with rocket-like tail fins, seats covered in red Naugahyde.

Sight—visual description—is the sense to which most writers default. Asked to describe my surroundings, I write what I see: "I am sitting in a wooden chair with five rounded ribs on the back. Simple and elegant, it could have been crafted by Shakers." The very act of writing this grounds me. I move into the story: "I bought this chair from a man with bright white hair and brown weathered skin, who sat cross-legged on the asphalt at the San Jose Flea Market—acres of parking lot, row upon row of secondhand and hand-me-downs, gently and roughly used. Furniture, appliances, clothing, and tools."

Sometimes an image grabs my attention, insisting that I describe what I see and write what it reminds me of. For example, I was sitting on a houseboat in the backwaters of Kerala, India. On the prow, the captain suddenly opened a bright green umbrella to shade himself from the sun. The surreal quality of the image made me flash back to a Magritte exhibition, with its paintings of men in bowler hats and floating green apples.

Then I remembered how I hadn't originally wanted to spend a night on a houseboat alone with three men—the captain, engineer, and cook. It felt a bit creepy. In fact, it turned out to be one of the highlights of my journey through India, a peaceful day of rest with my non-English-speaking crew, as we drifted across Lake Vembanad.

In this section you will find prompts that take you from your home to more exotic locales, from writing about the colors of a place to the effects of light.

1

You Ought to Be in Pictures

I WAS WRITING from memory about a trip I had taken to Indonesia more than twenty-five years ago. Like much of my writing, it was descriptive, but I knew details were missing—holes and shadows in my memories of almost three decades ago. This was my freewrite:

> The Dayak tribe emerged from the jungle as our small open boat put-putted past shallow reeds, pygmy palms, and shoreline scrub. Making our way down the muddy river in Borneo, I felt like Katherine Hepburn on the *African Queen*. John had persuaded me to see this tiny outpost where the Indonesian government planned to relocate farmers from overpopulated Java. He and his team of American scientists were evaluating whether rice could grow in the clay-like soil.
>
> Eight tribesmen led us single file into the humid jungle down a path they slashed with machetes as we trekked. In a clearing they felled slender saplings, and lashed them together to create a platform two feet off the ground for our tent. They meant to save us from trails of stinging red ants, but one afternoon their plans went awry.

One of my favorite prompts is "In this photo you are . . ." Write as if you are speaking to someone in the photo (it may be yourself). So I opened my photo album and saw my heavy orange backpack slung sedan-chair style over two poles carried by two tribesmen. The men who had met us wore shorts and shirts, topped by hats, no two alike—a jaunty straw sun hat with a cheerful red band, a black pork-pie, a wide-brimmed gaucho number, a policeman's hat, a Muslim prayer cap. They were all barefoot except for the man in the police cap. He wore an orange bomber jacket and black boots, despite the sticky heat. Maybe he really was the local police, as he claimed, even though there was no town, just two large communal houses on stilts, a bunkhouse built for the soil scientists, and a jerry-rigged cookhouse. A toothless crone in a photo gave me a lip-sucking grin. Perched on her head was a blanket folded into a large square, her entry into this Easter parade. A man was stoking the cooking fire, his sparse teeth blackened by a life of chewing beetle nuts, the blood-red juice pooling around his gums. I added these details to my story.

At one of my workshops at Book Passage, an independent bookseller in the Bay Area, a student brought a portrait of her family taken by a professional photographer when she was five. She had been blocked in her writing for over a year, but now, when she used the prompt "In this photo you are . . . ," the words came tumbling out. The freewrite became the prologue to a book about her mother, interspersed with the author's memories.

> In this one, Mama, you're smiling brightly, even though your shell is cracking. Dad's in shock. The rest of us don't know how to look. Can you really dress up and paste on a smile when the family is splitting apart? I'm too little to know. I stand on your lap, waving my fat arms, happy that we are all together for once. For once and for all,

I could say, with a ballooning feeling in my throat. Because this was the last time.

You were the only one who knew that, and yet you ordered the photographer to come, you laid our outfits out on our beds, you called Dad home from work on a Tuesday afternoon, and you made up your face as carefully as Ava Gardner. The funny thing is, you look radiant.

Maybe this is what you longed for: to get out. To fly the coop. Slip the collar, duck and run, vamoose, bugger off. You buggered off. You did a moonlight flit, even though it took you two years to accomplish it.

This photograph is your proof that you tried. You had us. You stuck with it—look at you!—five children, shiny with spit and terrified of losing something, though they know not what. You gave it your best, or so you told yourself. But you had to find out if there was something better. You had to know.

Did you ever find it, Mama? Did you ever find what you were looking for?

Another prompt that works well for photos is "What this photo doesn't show . . ."

In one of my Indonesian photos, I see myself wrapped in my blue sarong, cooling off near the stream by our campsite. What this photo doesn't show is that soon my body will be covered with sores from bathing in water used upstream as a latrine. What this photo doesn't show is that one day, John will say, "You have to leave."

Photos that seem standard-issue-bureaucratic, like those on a driver's license, passport, or military papers, may evoke memories and emotion. I remember every time I posed for a passport photo, and each of those days has a tale. My first passport picture is my favorite: me at nineteen, bright-eyed and innocent, with a shiny brown, shoulder-length flip. I still remember the white sleeveless dress with thin olive green stripes. I was about to leave for a year in Madrid and London, which would change my life forever.

At one workshop, a writer used her son's driver's license photo for this exercise and was moved to tears at the thought of his leaving for college.

In this photo you are a curly-haired youth, with a smile as wide as the world that lies open before you.

You are a child of moods like tides, born to a nature that feels everything, that struggles to control, understand, analyze, frame, make sense of the crazy world.

"This is what I call an intense baby," said the pediatrician when you were a few days old.

Intense about your frustrations, your triumphs: I sit! I stand! I read! I earn a black belt in Brazilian jujitsu! I will not submit! I will read the *Wall Street Journal* even though I am only ten years old!

Intense about your love, your territory. Defiant, beautiful, difficult, fire boy, muscle boy. "Look at these biceps, Mom!" Boy who gives a quick kiss on the cheek, boy who holds his secrets close, boy who scorns hippies and feeds stray cats. Boy who loves the world but hates to travel. My boy, tossing college acceptance letters on the table as if they mean nothing.

In this photo you are my curly-haired boy, about to fly away.

We learn a lot about the boy and his mother's love in this short freewrite with its poetic phrases and powerful imagery about her curly-haired boy, about to fly away: *a child of moods like tides, born to a nature that feels everything. Fire boy, muscle boy. Boy who loves the world but hates to travel.*

People often surprise us with what they use as prompts, and often surprise themselves with what comes out in their writing. In the next example, instead of a photo, a writer brought a drawing she had made of herself years earlier. She was working on a memoir about an abusive relationship, and this is what she wrote.

In this one you are angry and stunned. You thought you were just doing an exercise from the book *Drawing on the Right Side of the Brain*, a self-portrait. Just getting the details precisely right. Losing yourself in the shades and the light—drawing the line of the eyes, carefully marking each strand of hair separately as it curves down to your chin. The mouth not quite as wide as the width of the eyes, a flaw in the face that prevents real beauty, you think. So how did you not see what you were capturing as you darkened the space in between the lips, which are slightly parted? How did you miss the meaning behind the fixed gaze? The self-control evident somehow. As I look at you I can feel your jaws clenched; I know how tight you are in every part of your body. You are coiled but you don't know it. Seething energy ready to strike, but there is no direction outward. You can't let yourself see what is really happening, so you are angry at the world. You throw yourself into your work, are disgusted at the petty jealousies at the office, and you fight fight fight to get that promotion. But you don't see that the enemy is beside you in bed, is sitting doing scales on the electric guitar in front of the TV, is taking up too much space everywhere in the tiny apartment, is not letting you breathe.

Initially, the self-portrait reminds her of how tight and angry she was, and how she directed that anger into her work. Then, she has the stark realization that the enemy who is causing her unhappiness is beside her in bed.

EXERCISE

Choose a photo with one or more people in it. A photo with you in it is fine.

Do a freewrite with one of the following prompts:

1. Addressing someone in the photo: "In this photograph you are . . ."
2. Using your photo or one you conjure up from memory: "What this photo doesn't reveal is . . ."
3. Using your driver's license: "The day I went to have my picture taken"; "How my photo has changed over the course of my license renewals."

2

Seeing Is Believing

W HEN PEOPLE ARE first practicing freewrites I offer tangible subjects as prompts, such as "My Father's Car" or "My Childhood Bedroom." Some say the only requirement for being a writer is to have had a childhood. Just about everyone can describe their father's car or their childhood bedroom, and description is usually how people begin. Often, writers segue from description to memories or stories. This isn't calculated; it's what naturally emerges. In the examples below, look at how vibrant the writing can be, even if we focus just on visual description. Then notice how adding sound or touch enriches a piece. In each case, psychological underpinnings emerged for the writers effortlessly.

Dad's white 1958 Ford with rocket-like tail fins is seven years old, just like me.

"Be sure you have your galoshes," Mom reminds my brother and me, black umbrella hooked on her white gloved arm, her spike heels clicking on spring's drizzle-wet sidewalk towards the car. These are necessary accoutrements for our drive to New York City's First Church of Religious Science.

A thief once slashed the car's red convertible top when trying to break in. Dad ran out of the house to chase him away; the slash remained.

Mom sits in the front passenger seat; her white-gloved right hand holds aloft the open umbrella to protect her black beehive hairdo from rain coming through the slashed roof. She smokes an L&M with her ungloved hand while avoiding droplets from umbrella spikes.

Dad starts the engine with a smile. "The infinite spirit precedes us and makes our journey safe, happy, and prosperous. We are at the right place, at the right time, doing the right thing." We don't call this a prayer because Religious Science teaches that our thoughts will direct God by *treating* for something, not groveling in prayer.

Red Naugahyde chills my bare thighs beneath my dress. The thoroughfare's speeding gray slush splashes through a gaping rusted hole below my dangling red galoshes. I could fit through that hole. My heart races while I'm mesmerized by streaking slush below the car and wonder if I could fall through a moving car. I stop my scary thoughts, since negative thoughts might come true.

To distract myself I turn around onto my knees, waving at smiling faces of people who wave back from the cars behind us. Their faces blur behind windshield wipers and increasing rain. My younger brother uses an old red lipstick to draw stick-figure people and backwards letters on the car's side window. Seat belts have not been invented.

"My Father's Car" was the first freewrite topic I gave to the group, and this writer sprang out of the gate like a thoroughbred, writing as fast as she could. Visual details poured forth: the year and make of the car with its white body and slashed red top, her mother's black hair and white gloves, her own red galoshes. She paints the scene with images—the open umbrella, the rusted hole in the car floor. Details evoke an era—her mother with a beehive hairdo, smoking an L&M. Sound comes into play. We can hear her mother's spike heels clicking on the sidewalk and get a sense of who her father is from a line of dialogue. And touch. We feel the chill of the vinyl seat against the child's bare thighs and the splash of the speeding gray slush.

Another writer began his freewrite by describing his father's car, but almost immediately he told us volumes about his father and their relationship.

My father's car was a beige, mid-seventies Belvedere station wagon in which he spent what seemed like his entire life going to the dump (dragging me along with him), going to work, commuting an hour each way to the graveyard shift at the Santa Barbara IBM office, going to the bowling alley at least two or three times a week, taking us to the drive-in (before I got my own driver's license), where we would enjoy *Friday the 13th* triple horror features beginning at midnight, and, finally, as a stepping stone to roadside brawls where he would happily, and very efficiently, beat the living shit out of anybody unlucky and stupid enough to drive in less than a civilized manner, which could be anything from tailgating to participating in a traveling roadblock, and then attempt to defend such egregious behavior with typical, red-blooded American male aggression.

In another workshop, using the prompt "My Childhood Bedroom," a writer opened with a description of two white wooden beds, but I didn't anticipate what came next.

My childhood bedroom began with two white wooden beds, covered in white cotton bedspreads. The window, screened, looked out on the driveway where my dad parked a succession of cool Buick and Oldsmobile convertibles. He hid a bottle of vodka in the glove compartment, which I would empty and refill with water. In my bedroom, which began as our bedroom, we had matching beds for the first five years. When Janie got sick, Mother would change her dressings, putting the adhesive tape on the white headboard before placing it on the new gauze, over the punctures for drainage. They remodeled the house after she died, cutting our room in half, building a walk-in closet where her bed used to be. I could only sleep when it rained and the palm trees rustled.

The reference to her father's vodka gets our attention and the image of tape on the headboard stays with me, but I am really drawn in by the line "my bedroom, which began as our bedroom." Ours? I'm curious whom she's writing about. The mystery is solved, then she takes the piece to another level with the metaphor of cutting the room in half, building a closet where her sister's bed used to be. The person who wrote this is an experienced writer and therapist, yet she had never touched on this topic before or consciously thought about her sister's bed being replaced by a closet.

I've written using this prompt many times with my classes. In this excerpt, I moved beyond the description of the beds my sister and I slept in, with their red corduroy bedspreads and cotton ruffles printed with pink and red carnations, and touched on our relationship.

She was my worshipful baby sister, my roommate from the time she was three and I was nine, until I left for college. When she was in elementary school, she would try my persona on for size, slinging my purse over her shoulder, carrying my schoolbooks up the stairs to our room. At night, after lights-out, I entertained her with stories or shadow puppet shows on the wall behind our twin beds, where the light from the school across the street created our puppet stage. We laughed and talked until Dad yelled down the hall, "You girls better get to sleep in there!" We never turned in without our "kiss, hug, and secret" ritual—the secret a whispered "I love you" when we had nothing juicier to share.

EXERCISE

Here are two subjects you can describe or use as prompts to propel you into a story.

- My Father's Car.
- My Childhood Bedroom.

3

The Palette of Place

EVERYWHERE IN ITALY, I have taken notes, describing what I've seen. The silver-green olive groves of Puglia, where gnarled trees grow heavy with ripe black fruit. A Byzantine church in Ravenna that sparkles like the inside of a jewel box with its lapis lazuli mosaic ceiling strewn with gold stars—three thousand bits of glass per square yard.

On a drizzly afternoon in Venice, cold and gray, on the cusp of autumn and winter, I boarded a *vaporetto*, one of the city's waterbuses, to take me across the Grand Canal. As we plowed the sea-green water, past pink palazzos and creamy villas, a domed Palladian church emerged, ghostly, through the mist, floating above the waterline.

The palette of place infuses my experience. I am happy in Italy, where the colors, softened by time or design, are subtle and soothing, warm and alive.

My home in California is bathed in the colors I found there— sea green, umber, ocher, and a faded shade of brick the Italians call *mattone*. It wasn't a conscious decision to bring the Mediterranean home with me. I chose this palette long before I began to spend periods of time abroad, drawn to these colors because they made me feel good—peaceful, yet energized and creative.

I contrast this with my memories of East Berlin, when I traveled there in the sixties to see life on the other side of the Wall: a drab, gray city, a concrete barrier topped with barbed wire, an ominous guard tower near Checkpoint Charlie. People walked the streets unsmiling, heads down. I felt tired and empty. At the other end of the color spectrum, I remember visiting a gallery at San Francisco's Museum of Modern Art, where the canvases in bright reds and greens seemed to pop off the walls. They brought my energy up, but were too bold, too electric for my home.

Writing about the palette of place can create images in the mind as stunning as art or photography. Driving to her ancestral home in Sweden, this writer captures the landscape with its spare, graphic quality:

> In the distance I saw a handful of farm cottages painted oxblood red with windows trimmed in white. A rake and shovel leaned against the board-and-batten siding of a cabin with a pickup truck parked in front.

Later she describes the cabin where her great-grandfather lived. Although she doesn't name colors, she again conveys the spare, graphic elements, reinforced by a comparison of the house to a stick drawing. Because the color of the snowflakes is obvious, she doesn't need to fill it in.

> The cabin was a neat rectangle with a pitched roof, as simple as a child's stick drawing. A door in the middle of the facade was flanked on each side by a window. Three paper snowflakes with lacy cutouts taped inside one of the panes added the only touch of whimsy.

She contrasts the simple cabin with the interior of the manor house on the property:

> The living room was painted deep teal, and Oriental carpets covered the varnished wood floors. Hand-painted

blue and white tiles, similar to those in the royal palace at Drottningholm, covered the wood-burning stove in the corner of the room.

Color, like texture, temperature, and light, creates mood. In this example, deep teal creates a feeling of luxury, especially when juxtaposed with Oriental carpets and hand-painted tiles found at the royal palace.

When you write, think about the environments in which you place your characters. What colors are the walls, the furniture, the dishes? Is the garden thriving with colorful flowers or paved over with black asphalt? Is the sky blue or layered with steel-gray clouds announcing rain?

Notice the facts I incorporated into my notes on Italy and East Germany: The mosaic ceiling in Ravenna made of "three thousand bits of glass per square yard," "an ominous guard tower" at the Berlin Wall. I didn't simply say the church was beautiful or the wall was depressing.

The details move beyond meaningless adjectives, such as "beautiful" or "depressing," and add credibility. Describe the beauty; tell us what features made you feel depressed. Be specific, but not exhaustive, and incorporate facts subtly, so they don't call attention to themselves like billboards, breaking the mood, rhythm, or storyline.

Images help readers experience the place you're writing about—like the descriptions of the Palladian church floating above the water line, the gnarled olive trees, the Ravenna church that "sparkles like the inside of a jewel box."

EXERCISE

Try these writing prompts:

- Think of a location, whether city, town, or country-side. Describe the palette of the place.
- Think about images and details that would make the reader feel emotion and incorporate them in your description.

4

Local Color

F ROM IOWA TO ITALY, from Cannes to California's Central Valley, local ways offer local color, even in your own
backyard. Think of the details that define a place.

As we pulled into North English, Iowa, three old men in
rockers greeted us from the porch of the general store and
directed us to our destination. *Straight from Central Casting,*
I thought. In the places I've lived—New York, Chicago, Madrid, and London—you don't find general stores with pot-
bellied stoves, let alone old men rocking on the porch.

In California, it might be hip indie film directors playing
chess on the town plaza or women walking down the sidewalk in knee-length tights with their rolled yoga mats under
their arms. In rural India, it might be women in yellow saris,
entering homes jerry-rigged of blue plastic sheeting with cor-
rugated metal roofs. In Italy it might be a chef in whites pre-
senting a plate of homemade pasta, or this depiction by one
of my students of a rainy day in Venice:

> The gondoliers aren't singing now. It's a grim race
> against the deluge. A boatman unfolds a royal blue
> tarp and covers the fringed seats tourists have vacated;
> he throws his soggy Persian rugs on the stern to drain.
> When he detaches the *forcola,* the twisted wooden piece
> that holds his oar in place, I'm as startled as if he'd un-
> screwed a prosthetic arm and waved it in the air.

Watching the oarsman work, I temporarily push aside my own weather anxieties, fretting how he'll get to shore—fifteen feet of oily green water separate his boat from the banks of the canal.

One by one, gondolas glide into the next available stall, stringing together a slippery plank bridge to the dock. The craft bob up and down in the restless water, like ebony piano keys played by invisible fingers. The black wooden boats are varnished with rain, but the gondolier steps across their rolling prows, a Venetian Jesus walking on water.

I especially like the details and images describing the gondolas: black wooden boats varnished with rain, jumping like ebony piano keys; the fringed seats and soggy Persian rugs. I can see the forcola, when the gondolier unscrews it and holds it aloft. But what really grabs me is the image of the oarsman stepping across the bobbing prows.

To practice coming up with details and images that define a place, try this exercise: Describe a place so that we can guess where you're writing about, but don't use clichés. For example, for Venice you might say "Renaissance palazzos in dreamy pastels rise from the canal in this city without roads" instead of "Gondoliers sang 'O sole mio.'" If you're doing this in a group, write about places the others might know. The guessing game doesn't work for places that are too unfamiliar.

EXERCISE

Use these prompts:

- What details and images distinguish the place where you live or a place you've visited? You can write a list or do a freewrite.

- For the game mentioned in this chapter, choose a place that might be familiar to your circle of writers and describe it with enough detail so that they can guess where it is when you read it aloud, but without using clichés that give it away.

5

Our Homes, Ourselves

O UR HOMES REFLECT who we are and affect how others perceive us. The details convey character, personality, and history far better than adjectives or labels. For example, in *The Amazing Adventures of Kavalier & Clay,* the author Michael Chabon shows us instead of telling us that Rosa is an avant-garde artist by describing her room.

> There was something exultant about the mess that Rosa had made. Her bedroom-studio was at once the canvas, journal, museum, and midden of her life. She did not "decorate" it; she infused it. Sometime around four o'clock that morning, for example, half disentangled from the tulle of a dream, she had reached for the chewed stub of a Ticonderoga she kept by her bed for this purpose. When, just after dawn, she awoke, she found a scrap of loose-leaf paper in her left hand, scrawled with the cryptic legend "lampedusa." . . . Socks, blouses, skirts, tights, and twisted underpants lay strewn across teetering piles of books and phonograph albums, the floor was thick with paint-soaked rags and chromo-chaotic cardboard palettes, canvases stacked four deep stood against the walls. She had discovered the surrealist potential of food, about which she had rather pioneeringly complicated emotions, and everywhere lay portraits of broccoli stalks, cabbage heads,

tangerines, turnip greens, mushrooms, beets—big, colorful, drunken tableaux that reminded Joe of Robert Delaunay.

He tells us the room is a mess, but then he shows us the canvas, journal, museum, and midden of her life. How wonderful to move from the superficiality of "decoration" to the deeper "infusion." He gives us specifics, such as clothes strewn over piles of books, paint-soaked rags, and surreal portraits of food, to show—not tell—us that Rosa is an artist, creative and messy.

In his memoir, *Getting Personal*, Phillip Lopate lets us know his parents by describing their Pocket Books collection—the very name of this paperback series pinpoints an era. Notice the details: cellophane-peeling covers, browning pages that would crack if you bent the corners, the kangaroo logo.

> My parents had a bookcase which held a few hardcovers and a library of Pocket Books, whose flimsy, browning pages would crack if you bent down the corners. I can still picture those cellophane-peeling covers with their kangaroo logo, their illustrations of busty, available-looking women or hard-bodied men or solemn, sensitive-looking Negroes; with titles like *Intruder in the Dust, Appointment in Samarra, Tobacco Road, Studs Lonigan, Strange Fruit, Good Night, Sweet Prince, The Great Gatsby, The Sound and the Fury.*

All the senses can come into play when you describe your home. At one of my workshops, a mother of four boys described the smell of dirty socks that pervaded her home, and a world traveler wrote about her baskets and pottery. As you'll see in the later section on touch, the fabrics we use to deco-

rate our homes can also reveal a lot about us—from our upholstery to the sheets we choose.

In the following example, which began in class as a freewrite with the topic "Spring Cleaning," a self-proclaimed neat
freak gave us a tour of her home and her psyche.

I usually begin my spring cleaning with my pencil cup.
With laserlike focus I test each pencil, pen, and highlighter to see if they still have what it takes to remain a
tenant in the cup. Parker ballpoint black pen, ink running a bit spotty—you're history! Red Sharpie, looking
pale and weak—it's over. Faded yellow highlighter, I see
you hiding behind the BIC Matic Grip Pencil—into the
trash you go. Oh, stop begging, your days are over and
you know it! I show no mercy as I diligently ready my
pencil cup for the season ahead, prepared to write pithy
and powerful prose, sign cashable checks, and doodle
during boring conference calls.

Brimming with clean-pencil-cup energy, I stride con-
fidently to my clothes closet. Glancing inside I cannot
believe that my wardrobe is in this much disarray, again.
I pick up a pair of black pants lying crumpled at my feet,
entangled in a three-way with my running shoes and a
small gold evening bag. "Do you like living like this?"
I chastise my pants. Too embarrassed to answer, they
do not reply. Even worse, several shirts have managed
to migrate (on their own, it seems to me) from the dor-
mant "fall-winter" closet down the hall to my active
"spring-summer" closet. "All right," I tell myself, "don't
panic, just start pairing up socks and putting them back
where they belong and no one will get hurt." After two
hours of sorting and sifting, my clothes closet is at last
spring-clean certified.

Proud of her accomplishments, she flings open her garage door and flattens the "self-satisfied smirks" off the faces of a "posse of cardboard boxes." And then she finds her epiphany: that the process is unending and she likes it that way, because it allows her to shape her story through what she chooses to keep.

Little by little the stuff of the universe finds its way into my life. The 1950s vintage rhinestone pin I saw at a garage sale and simply had to have, the adorable little black dress that whispered "Take me home, I'm stylish and fifty percent off," the Costco fifty-pack special of ballpoint pens. As I settle these newly acquired treasures into their closets and cupboards, I conclude that we clean freaks are fighting a losing battle. It seems to be a law of nature that the organized shall become disorganized, and the empty turn to full.

Just as artists create their worlds with paint and canvas, I shape the story of my life in part through this process of choosing what I keep and what I clean out.

I love the personification of "stuff" and the humor that runs through this piece. I laugh at her conversation with her pants and the idea of wiping self-satisfied smirks off the cardboard boxes in her garage. The pace of the writing conveys the energy of the author as she whirls through her spring cleaning. I can picture her testing and tossing her pens, doodling during conference calls, marching to her closet, eyeing her boxes suspiciously. The freewrite began as a riff on spring cleaning. She didn't realize her epiphany until she reread the freewrite.

My home tells you that I am a traveler and a lover of art. "Collector of fine hand-loomed textiles" has a nice ring. I had no idea I was a fabric addict until I traveled to Bali and began buying batik sarongs and hand-loomed ikats. Functional art. What could be better? I met with weavers and antique dealers, went to open-air markets and remote villages. I ended up shipping two crates home. Not that I exactly had a home. At the time, I rented a flat filled with secondhand furniture. The textiles stayed in storage for nearly ten years.

Then at last I bought a home—a place that became my canvas for artistic expression. I broke the ikats out of their crates and had cushions made for a banquette in my remodeled kitchen. I draped an antique piece from the island of Flores across the arm of the sofa in my office. I upholstered my home with my memories.

EXERCISE

Writing prompts:

- What does your home say about you?
- Describe how the colors in a room of your house make you feel. Why did you choose them?
- What story does that room tell?

6

Drawing Home

S OMETIMES IT'S A RELIEF to let go of words and let crayons or colored pencils do the talking. Don't worry, no artistic talent required. Just the willingness to take a memory journey to a house or apartment you lived in at a time you'd like to write about. This drawing exercise can quiet the mind, while bringing out vivid memories and stories.

One student drew her room at a Zen monastery in the Ventana Wilderness, east of Carmel, California. Her freewrite, which we dubbed "Menopausal Monk," begins with a description as she warms up to write about her suffering.

For three months the world left me alone in my little monk's cell. A heated dorm room with a cot, a bureau, and a makeshift desk, where I sat on the floor before a low Japanese table.

For three months I counted the days until I'd get to go home and off this god-awful schedule—I had to wake up at 3:15 A.M. in order to have time to drink my coffee and read *The New Yorker*. But even though I counted the days to return home, this was my home for a time, and now it is a place I long for.

In that room I lay on my cot and all night the river roared outside my window, swelling from lazy stream to churning brown torrent as the autumn deepened.

In that room I shut my door and no one bothered me,

no phone, no e-mail. I sat at my tiny desk and wrote for hours whenever I didn't have to be in the zendo or at my job cleaning the bathhouse. I was in there alone with such intensity that the monk across the hall told me later she thought I might be doing voodoo.

In that room I lay on the floor and sobbed, day after day, as my midlife hormones surged in fiery fluctuations, over and over telling the zendo manager my little story, why, once again, I hadn't made it to my cushion.

This short freewrite is rich with emotion. The details reveal her character (a monk who needs coffee and *The New Yorker* before meditating), adding tension and humor—her comforts contrasted with the routine of the monastery. Without planning a metaphor, one sprang out: the churning brown river reflects her emotional state. Then, a twist, as we learn she lay on the floor sobbing, and an intimate revelation.

EXERCISE

For this exercise I like to use a large sheet of newsprint, so that the drawing can be expansive and I can jot down memories or story ideas with a catch phrase as they arise, but 8 ½ x 11 paper is also fine.

First, draw the floor plan of a house, as if you were looking down on it from above, like an architect's blueprint. Sketch the skin of the house, all the rooms and hallways. Add details like furniture, carpets, fireplaces, and lamps. Draw a plan of each floor if there is more than one.

Now picture yourself traveling to the house. Are you in a car, exiting the highway? Have you taken the train from another city and a cab from the station? Or are you climbing the stairs out of the subway, walking down the sidewalk to your building, and taking the elevator to your apartment?

Enter the front door and walk through the house or apartment, then settle into whichever room you choose. Feel yourself in the room. What time of day is it? Once in the house, do you turn on a light? How old are you? Write whatever story arises. If no story percolates up for you, describe the room and describe yourself in that room. What are you doing? Is anyone else there?

7

Let There Be Light

THE QUALITY OF LIGHT and the movement and temperature of air or water add emotional content to a scene. Think how it feels to be in a cold, damp, dark home or one where a warm breeze drifts from room to room. Consider the moods created by a sunlit field of red poppies in Provence, the glare of fluorescent lights in an airless Wall Street office, or swans floating on a pond at twilight.

Late one afternoon, as I drove from Albuquerque to Taos, the sky was dark in the distance. When I arrived at my destination, I did a freewrite of my experience.

> I was driving in a color world—peachy earth and sea foam–green desert scrub—with a backdrop that looked like a black-and-white photo. Suddenly, a torrential downpour broke and I was in darkness. The sky cracked open with a jagged yellow neon flash. I was driving straight toward lightning, and wondered whether I might die.

When I've had my fill of Sturm und Drang, I can transport myself to a warm, sunny place, by thinking of this scene in Tahiti.

> In the warm aqua waters, I float between two palm-studded islands. Lying on my back in a red bikini, I am

reading a paperback novel, rocking on Peter's blue plastic air mattress, anchored in the lagoon by a rope tied to a heavy stone. Suddenly, I feel a cool splash as Peter, an Aussie with thick black-framed glasses, pops up at my side.

"Cigarette?" he offers.

In the seventies this was not a faux pas. Still, I decline.

"Iced tea? Lemonade? Gasohol?"

We were at Club Med Mooréa, where, each afternoon, guests slathered in suntan oil scooped their cups into a vat of wine swill, sometimes dipping down so deep they submerged their greasy forearms into the liquid. The wine glistened with oil-slick rainbows.

"No, thank you."

He dove deep with his Barney Google eyes and waited on the shore until the lunch bell rang.

If I go back to my childhood, my quiet place is under the beech tree in my family's backyard, where the light screened dappled through the leaves.

My father had cut out the bottom branches, shaping a cubbyhole where I could lie with Louisa May Alcott and her little women—Meg, Jo, Amy, and Beth—eager to know who would marry Laurie. As I sipped my iced tea, I had definite opinions at the age of nine. "No, Jo, don't marry old Professor Baer! Marry Laurie. Don't open a school for boys! Have your own children like Meg." I identified with parts of each sister—Meg's motherly instincts, Jo's writing, Amy's artistic nature, Beth's quietness.

Under the beech tree, I was in heaven. The breeze was soft and warm. I could hear the hum of a lawn mower, smell the sweetness of fresh cut grass. The light was clear, a cloudless afternoon, as leaf patterns danced on the pages. Later my mother would insist I go door to door selling Girl Scout cookies. I hated selling. I hated being a Girl Scout. But I loved chocolate mint cookies.

In the next excerpt, written by one of my students in class, note the references to light and temperature: winter light, standing lamp, cold black glass. The shift from day to night creates an emotional turning point even in this short freewrite.

I sit on my window seat often, but never to talk with my friends. This is my alone space, my nook in the dormer window, looking over the backyard, the ravine, the neighbors' houses, and, far away below in the distance, the lights coming on in Boston. When the trees are bare like this, in their shades of buff and gray, it seems I could almost see into forever, into my future, the waiting city after the safety of the garden and the suburbs.

In the fading winter light I wait before I turn on my standing lamp. I want to see all the shades of light before I wash them away with my lamp and turn my broad view into flat, cold black glass through which I can only see other lights.

But even then the window seat has its charm, in its snug, shut-in quality. I see the white curtains framing the window, notice the sounds of my family downstairs. But the balance is somehow wrong now. From a cozy vantage point on the world, a place to plot outside adventure, my window seat has become the retreat of the timid, the unsociable. The dark glass makes it feel cold. I stand up and look around my room one more time, then turn off the light and walk down the stairs.

In the Dutch masters' paintings, light is like a character. At the Frick Collection in New York, a painting by Johannes Vermeer reveals an intimate interior flooded with golden light. The audio guide explains:

> Whatever the nature of the human exchange depicted here, it soon seems obvious that the real subject of the picture is light—the intangible light shown bursting in through the open window, breaking up reflections in the leaded panes, muffled through the curtains, caressing the soft plaster wall, lingering sporadically on glowing fabrics, sparkling glass, or the soft expanse of the vellum map. . . . But the light recedes into dark corners and will soon accent the young woman's beguiling face and soft kerchief differently. In this subtle fashion, Vermeer makes light a metaphor for time, and reminds us ever so gently of its inevitable consequences.

In the following example, the writer has hiked to the top of a hill and, looking down at the valley, focuses on blocks of color—green trees below, white clouds above—rather than on the objects themselves. The tricks of light remind her of the mysteries of life and death, and make her wonder whether, in fact, they are separate.

> Green on the bottom, white on top
> Life and death, adjacent, inseparable
> Oh, wait! The green and white were just tricks of the
>   light
> Oh, wait! Life and death were just tricks of the light

Sit comfortably with your pen and paper nearby. Inhale deeply and then exhale slowly. Follow your breath, in and out. Slow and deep. Relax your shoulders, neck, back, abdomen, hands, and feet. Keep your breathing slow and regular.

Now think of a place where you felt safe and relaxed. Perhaps a place you recall from your childhood where you felt comfortable, at ease. Or a place you went on vacation where you were able to relax. Are you outdoors or in a particular room? What time of year is it? What do you look like? Are you standing, sitting, lying down? Are you alone or with others?

Now think about your sensations. What do you see, feel on your skin, hear, smell, taste?

What is the light like?

See yourself in this scene, then tell us what happens. Do you move? Say something? Think something? What changes? This exercise often works best if you write in the present tense. Write whatever comes up.

8

Art Scene

S TROLLING THROUGH CHRISTIE'S auction preview, my
six-year-old nephew, Eli, revealed a sharp critical eye and
straightforward formula for evaluating art. He stood before
a wall-sized Rothko examining two rectangles—one lemon-
lime, one orange—hovering on a yellow field.

"Estimated price, fifteen to twenty million dollars!" he exclaimed. He quickly did the math. "That's five million dollars
per color!"

Sometimes I go to a museum with a writing buddy and we
take turns sitting before a painting, giving each other prompts,
writing for ten minutes and reading our work to each other.
Sometimes I go by myself. With my notebook in hand and art
surrounding me, I don't feel alone.

On a visit to San Francisco's Museum of Modern Art with
a group of writers, I found inspiration in every gallery. Not
from the facts about the art or artist, but rather from my response to the art.

There are many ways to approach art as a prompt. You can
describe what you see. You can write from your life, whatever
is triggered by the topic or the art. Or you can write fiction.

Much of the art we saw that day was minimalist, entire
canvases of just one color. I offered the prompt "Down to
the Essence." In response, one person wrote about editing a
story.

Pared down, strong. I will take out all the extra words. Adverbs, adjectives, and equivocations. Dreary dead language, uncommitted, uncertain.

Boiled down to a strong brew of excellent flavor. Vibrant, simple, clear as clean water.

It won't matter how long it took—all the rejects, false starts, discarded drafts like scraps of fabric strewn on the floor, the cut-outs, the hems, the sheared-off seams. Give me the dress, finished, ironed, and just the right size.

The idea of editing down to the bones was a perfect analogy to the art on view. Her other images were equally apt and vivid—*boiled down to a strong brew, clear as clean water.* How great to compare writing and editing to sewing, with its false starts and cutting away what doesn't belong. The final image of the dress is tight and satisfying: *finished, ironed, and just the right size.*

When we moved into a gallery of Andy Warhol's paintings, I recalled his line about everyone having fifteen minutes of fame. If you use a Warhol painting as a prompt, you might want to write about those fifteen minutes. Another prompt came to mind: What would your life be like if you suddenly became famous? If you write fiction, imagine what it would be like if one of your characters suddenly became famous. How would the character cope?

In this freewrite at the museum, an author of children's storybooks spoke through the voice of her character:

If I were famous, I would handle the crowd. Give me control, give me power, give me everything I deserve!

Admiration and lots of compliments. Money, too.

And houses everywhere. On the beach in Hawaii and a big rolling ranch in Wyoming with chestnut horses galloping all over the place.

Famous, world famous! Take my picture, tell me more. How great, how amazing. I deserve it all. Big pictures of my face hanging on the wall, with backgrounds in radiant colors.

Dwell on me, pour out your praise. What then? Is there an empty time, when the people go to sleep? Wake them up! I need another dose. More clapping, please. Feed my ego, keep me high. Louder, brighter, faster, shinier, richer, denser, more emphatic. Not a little famous—the most! Why else be alive? What's the use of being part of a crowd, a miserable mortal, one of seven billion? Give it to me, the most special and amazing, the most deserving and remarkable, the most famous and fabulous, the immortally splendiferous princess of the world.

I can see her bossy royal character, as if in an animated film, bursting with a child's enthusiasm—*famous and fabulous, more clapping, please.* But the adult writer lets us know what she really thinks of all this. *Louder, brighter, faster, shinier, richer, denser, more emphatic.* We're over the top. Although her children's books deal with emotionally complex subjects, if she adapts this freewrite for a young audience, she may change phrases like "Feed my ego, keep me high" and eliminate repetition. But if she'd tried to wordsmith it as she did this freewrite, she would have squelched the energy, inspiration, and freedom to explore.

In another gallery, Frank Stella's colorful three-dimensional works prompted me to write about a time I felt giddy. Alexander Calder's mobiles were art in motion. They prompted me to write about being in balance, taking a chance.

You get the idea. You can describe what you see literally or take it to a metaphoric level and write about what the piece symbolizes or the emotion it triggers in you.

In a room full of sculptures, our group of writers used the prompt "Taking Up Space."

Some things take up more space than they deserve. People are like that—they barge into a room, changing the mood, the direction, throwing energy everywhere.

The writer goes on to compare humans with animals:

I prefer the pileated woodpecker on his dead tree, recycling insects. Use what you need, no more. But then again, a chipmunk never imagined a hollow sculpture like this one, floating upside down, lace-like lattice. Even the bowerbird's art is for a purpose—to catch the girl. Only a human is so foolish, so brain-inflicted, to hang a mobile or fill a courtyard with sculpture, taking up space, invading the world with our presence.

EXERCISE

Look at a painting or piece of sculpture in a museum, art gallery or park, your home—anywhere you find it. If you don't have access to the actual works of art, use a photo of a painting in a book or on a postcard. Let a prompt float up, then grab a pen (some museums allow only pencils in the galleries) and write for ten minutes. This exercise is fun to do with a friend. If you're in a museum, move on to another gallery, and take turns choosing different pieces of art and giving each other writing prompts.

9

Writing on the Road

To capture the details of place, dialogue, and your
own emotions, take notes. That's what I learned from
Frances Koltan, the travel editor at *Mademoiselle* magazine
when I was a guest editor there after college. She encouraged
me to write down phrases, descriptions, and impressions in
the moment.

As we rode a bus through Mexico City, she asked to see my
notes. I had jotted down the names of plants and flowers, his-
torical details, and images that impressed me. I later incorporated them into my article.

On one of our excursions, I wrote about the landscape: "On
the road to Texcoco, the land is dry, and scattered plantings
catch my eye. There are cactus and red pepper trees, fields of
corn and emerald-green seas of alfalfa. A mule team draws a
plow through fields that are fringed by telephone poles."

In another scene, I described the faithful approaching the
shrine of the Virgin of Guadalupe on their knees. "A child carries gladioli. A man spreads out newspaper pages so that his
wife will not scrape her knees." Today, I might snap a photo
to remind me of details, though I don't want a camera to keep
me from thinking about how I feel when I'm there.

Throughout the trip, I recorded unusual phrases in my notebook as soon as I heard them, like the comment—intended as
a compliment—made by a Mexican host when our group arrived: "I've never seen such a chunk of beauty."

Susan Orlean, the author of the bestsellers *The Orchid Thief* and *Rin Tin Tin*, agrees—she jots down quotes as soon as possible. But when she's working on a story she doesn't take notes right away. Instead, she focuses on establishing relationships with people and taking everything in. Like many travel writers, she writes her recollections at the end of the day, while the details are still fresh.

The travel writer Tim Cahill recommends taking contemporaneous notes when you're seeing something for the first time: "You have to sit there for a while, ten or fifteen minutes," he says, "to get the commonplace observations out. Then you're writing sentences and getting in touch with your feelings. You think of the exterior landscape—what it is—and the interior landscape—how it makes you feel." Cahill discovers what the experience means by writing about it.

There's a balance. If you have a great memory, you can get away with less note taking and type up the day's events in the evening. Either way, a small notebook and pen will serve you well when you're on the road. I always have one with me, even when I'm close to home.

In one of my notebooks, I found my writing from a trip to India. As I observed the passing landscape at the time, I thought about how to put it into words. In my notebook I wrote: "White sap dripping down smooth tree trunks, rows of silent sentries in the shadowed woods." The words instantly took me back to that day.

The white Ambassador sedan wound from the Arabian Sea to India's Cardamom Hills, past cacao, pineapple, and tea plantations; an elephant with his mahout; and sacred cows lounging in the center of the road. We paused on a bridge overlooking a vast plain with a river running through it, where village women kneaded their laundry on broad, flat stones. Two girls, balancing bundles of twigs on their heads, scampered barefoot along a stream that split like the veins on the back of my hand.

The road darkened as we entered the shadowy forest of a rubber plantation. The word "sentries" sprang to mind, as I observed the trees, straight and watchful, planted in rows. The smooth trunks wore sky-blue plastic skirts, short and flared, like young girls twirling at an ice skating rink. These wraps hovered over the wounds where trees had been tapped to draw off the sap.

I could simply have written: "We drove through a rubber plantation." But what would a reader see? So I asked myself how I would describe this to someone who had never traveled to such a place, and looked carefully at the images and details.

The simile of the stream splitting like the veins on the back of my hand came to me as my eyes shifted from the stream to my hand. I contemplated the blue plastic "skirts" on the trees and thought about what simile might convey what I saw—twirling young ice skaters, I decided.

When I write I pay attention not only to the facts but also to the rhythm and sound of the words. In this case, I liked the visual and tactile image of white sap dripping down the smooth trunk, and felt that the alliterative simile "silent sentries in shadowed woods" added a poetic quality to the scene.

Another excerpt from that travel notebook reminds me of the day I listened for hours to "the rain on the car roof, a calm, consistent patter."

In a driving rain, we park and walk back over the bridge that crosses the river that bisects the town. An elderly woman drags her body after me, her atrophied, twisted legs following her torso, which follows her arms, scrambling to reach me, my face, her hand thrust up towards me. I avert my eyes. "Nay, nay." I am so used to saying, "No, leave me alone" to the beggars and touters. My driver indicates that this one should receive alms. We walk back to the car and I give him money to bring to her.

Throughout the journey, I noted down what I saw. Maybe I'll incorporate some of these images or details into future pieces.

- An old woman with three goats ambles down the rutted, one-lane road, sidestepping puddles. Her flat breasts hang down to her waist.
- The bare-chested rubber-maker wearing a pink plaid sarong. He presses the rectangle of white rubber through a wringer, then hangs it on the clothesline to dry.
- My driver in his crisp white safari shirt and trousers. The plastic Virgin Mary on the dashboard.

From a rubber plantation to a mall near home, notes written in the moment have vitality and specificity that make readers feel they're in the scene. You can do it as a freewrite or simply jot down phrases. The important thing is to capture in real time or shortly thereafter what your senses have taken in.

EXERCISE

Choose an outdoor scene and describe it with such specificity that we can see it, or even feel we're there. Describe the people. What are they wearing, doing, saying? Incorporate dialogue. You are always free to shift to memory or story or stay with describing the scene. Try to come up with at least one simile.

10

Playing with a Full Deck

A T A WRITING WORKSHOP in Santa Cruz, overlooking the Pacific Ocean, each participant drew a tarot card. Most of us knew nothing about how to read the deck, but we had no trouble using the words and images on them as prompts. We jumped right in, using the cards to say what was on our minds in the moment.

One writer drew a card called the Royal Maze. Musing on how to structure her second novel, she used the maze as a symbol of writing.

Writing a novel is a tangle with decisions about direction to be made on every lap of the journey. The question of where and how to enter the maze can be so difficult as to be crippling. For some people the answer is to start anywhere and then, once the story has begun to unfold, to go back and find the optimum point of entrance. With my first novel I started on the outside of the maze and hacked my way in by starting at the beginning and writing hundreds of pages that I ended up lopping off. This time I'd like to make a helicopter landing right into the middle of things and take it from there. The name "royal maze" is a reminder that any subject can be worthy of attention. The illustration looks like a target, reminding me that every story has a center: a pivotal action or decision, often erroneous, that throws things into a state of imbalance that must be resolved. This central action creates instability in the lives of the characters but functions, inside the story, as a prime motor, a beating heart of the whole operation. It's a mistake, perhaps, or a misunderstanding that may lead to happy resolution or to tragedy. It doesn't really matter. What counts is that the steps of the story must be as strongly interdependent as the three linked metal rings at the top of the card.

You can also do this exercise with a regular deck of playing cards. Draw a card and see what thoughts pop into your mind. The number on the card may remind you of yourself at that age or the address of a house you lived in. Hearts may trigger stories of love or heartbreak, diamonds may make you think of engagement rings or South African mines or linoleum patterns on the floor. We did this at a workshop I led, and people were surprised by the words that came from their pens.

A person who drew the four of clubs began with enthusiasm: "I love four!" Think of the fours that have meaning to you: the four directions, four-leaf clover, Four Noble Truths, four seasons.

Another drew the two of hearts and wrote in a very different tone:

As my partner and I age I have begun to worry about how much time we have left together. I don't even want to imagine how life would be without her. I remember the 1989 earthquake. We were in a Safeway on Ocean Avenue that had townhouses built on top. As the canned goods began hitting the floor and bouncing down the aisle, the building swayed and a can of peas almost brained me. It was clear to me the building would give way and we were done for. I was at peace because I thought we would die together.

A third wrote more generally about family games:

I hate playing cards. My family played cards so they wouldn't have to talk about anything meaningful. Drink highballs and giggle. Stay in the box, fill the room with cigarette smoke so we couldn't see the world.

EXERCISE

1. If you have a tarot deck, draw one of the archetypes and write whatever comes up for you.
2. If you use a regular deck of playing cards, place the cards face down and draw one. Turn it over and write whatever comes up.

PART TWO

Sound

IN THE VILLAGES OF BALI I listened to the gamelan, the cymbals, and the bells. On a prairie in Nebraska I heard a train chug by, its plaintive whistle *whoo-hoo* wailing. Near the track, cows mooed and moaned. In a nursery, a baby cooed.

The sounds of nature soothe me—from waves crashing on the rocky coast to wind soughing through the trees. The sounds of the city assault me—I clap my hands to my ears as a fire engine passes, its high-pitched siren screaming. On the sixth-floor of a New York City apartment building, I cringe under the covers when the predawn garbage trucks rattle cans and grind their grist.

Bells and whistles, cries and whispers. Sound fills a void in writing that we sometimes don't realize exists.

11

The Sounds of My Childhood

I REMEMBER THE SOUNDS of summer, growing up on Long Island: the lawnmower's thrum, the screen door slamming like gunshot, a baseball announcer soothing radio listeners with a play-by-play. In winter, a storm door replaced the screen door. I recall the smack as it closed, the squeaky crunch of my rubber boots walking on snow. Bonfires crackling, teakettles whistling, the *click-click-click* of the keys of my old Smith-Corona portable typewriter. I can hear the clatter of silverware as my sister set the kitchen table for dinner, while Vivaldi and Bach offered solace on the living-room stereo. When I moved to California, I missed the thunder—the deep timpani of my childhood—until, thirty years later, there came a season of thunder and lightning.

Listen to how verbs and onomatopoeic nouns convey sound—*thrum, smack, crackle, whistle, click,* and *clatter*.

Sounds are a way into our experience, a demarcation of place. A writer raised on a farm thinks of heifers baying, while one who lived in a one-bedroom apartment with parents at each other's throats remembers the sound of heated anger. Ask yourself, what does a baying heifer sound like? What is the sound of heated anger? Go a level deeper, to the low and moo of the cow in the barn, to the hiss and snap of angry words.

In this freewrite, a student begins with concrete sounds, then shifts to moods evoked by sounds.

The sounds of my childhood are the barking of beagles, banging of screen doors, crickets at night, the Beatles and Joni Mitchell and Joan Baez.

The sounds are dark and light, depending on my mother's moods, which are pain or joy. This is life with a bipolar mother who is the center of the world.

Some mornings, the sobbing, the shouts of rage, the crash of an object hitting the kitchen wall. The calm and steady voice of my father trying to bring reason, like a bucket dipped in the vast, wave-crashed surf of her unhappiness.

Other days—the notes of Mozart, smell of bacon, birds in the yard outside. Where are the birds on the bad days? Do they hide away, like my brothers and me, burrowing deeper into the nests of our covers, afraid to come out? Do they only sing when the sun shines, when music plays and bacon sizzles, when the coast is clear?

Another writer, now in her forties, recaptured the carefree feeling of childhood summers in Boston.

The days made a hum, a steady background sound of distant traffic and fans and refrigerators running in all the houses in the neighborhood. Other noises came and went: the *snickety-snick* of rotary lawnmowers, the *whoosh* of sprinklers starting up, and the soft rattle when the spray fell on leaves. Some days the drone of cicadas seemed deafening; other days, engrossed in games with the neighborhood kids, I would hardly hear them at all.

With onomatopoeic words like *snickety-snick* and *whoosh*, she brings the scene alive.

I compare the sounds of my Long Island childhood to the

sounds of my life in California. Here, in the San Francisco Bay Area, we don't have storm doors. Typewriters are consigned to museums. After years of drought, lawns may not be environmentally correct, so we're more likely to hear the whir and scream of leaf blowers.

Birds warble in the West as they did in the East, but sometimes their song is chased by crows cawing, their vocal chords rusted by car exhaust. They sound stressed, as if they might be calling out for WD-40.

EXERCISE

Use the following writing prompts:

1. The Sounds of My Childhood.
2. The worst sound of all was . . .
3. The best sound of all was . . .

12

Wherever Music Takes You

As I approached the Golden Gate Bridge on my way out of town, I cranked up Willie Nelson singing "On the Road Again." A song of freedom, here we go! By the time I was midway across the span, I was waltzing in the driver's seat to the dreamy sounds of "Georgia," symbolically telling the world "I'm on my way; don't bother me."

When I compiled this audiotape (those were the days of tapes), I had matched the lineup to the scenery along the coast. I felt like a psychologically savvy techno genius for having made a tape where the music was so perfectly synced with the landscape and my mood.

Years later, at a lunch with Georgia Hesse, the former travel editor of the *San Francisco Examiner*, I discovered that she had elevated matching music and place to new levels of refinement. Georgia knows a lot about music, and one day she decided to write about how she creates a personal soundtrack for the passing scenery.

On a warm midsummer morning, a friend and I celebrated our day-old, laser-red, CD-equipped Mustang convertible, curving through a tangle of oak forest on the Lake Berryessa hills north of San Francisco. As we crested the grade, Charlotte Church hit her highest notes: "And thine is the *king-dom* . . . and the *pow-er* and the *glor-eey,* forev-*er. . . .*"

No tremor shook the trill; no wobble, no waver in a soprano as clear and flawless as the sky.

We changed the CD and so the mood. Rolling on back roads, heading north, we swung onto old Highway 99W. Count Basie jammed with Duke Ellington: "Take the A Train" and "Jumpin' at the Woodside." We beat time and munched fast food as we cruised all alone while trucks thundered by on intense Interstate 5 off to the west. So cool, so American; you make me feel so young.

Later, more solemnly, we wound around Lassen Peak with violin sonatas saluting the higher, thinner air: Mozart to match the mountain.

In Idaho on the heights above the Snake River, we felt the first pelts of rain and stood rim-side to watch a storm approach with the inevitability of the fourth movement of Beethoven's Symphony No. 7. I longed for that music. Next time.

Snowstorm on the North Rim, sun that would scorch a lizard on the South Rim: in fair weather or foul, no companion so complements the Grand Canyon as Ferde Grofé's "Grand Canyon Suite." It paints the scenery with sound. Maybe only an American composer can create such a sense of space; most classical Europeans seem more comfortable in parlors than on the wild prairie.

Perhaps no master gives voice to the natural world that surrounds him as does Jean Sibelius. Bleak, remote, full of myths and mysteries, his works, especially "Finlandia," recall to memory that spare and haunting landscape at the chilly top of Europe. He is right at home, also, on the serpentine, alpine Going-to-the-Sun Road, the only route across the million acres of Glacier National Park.

Not only does music pair well with the landscape; it conjures up scenes in our minds. Sometimes I'll play a recorded compilation at a workshop and ask students to write the scenes they imagine. For example, after a few notes of "Caravan," first recorded in 1936 by the Jazzopators with Duke Ellington on piano, writers are pounding out smoky nightclub scenes, their characters dancing wildly and tossing back drinks. When "Quando m'en vo," Puccini's plaintive aria from *La Bohème*, begins, they quickly switch gears. Even if they don't understand the words, they have no problem creating melodramatic dialogue that matches the soprano's emotional intensity.

EXERCISE

Use the following prompts:

1. Play a piece of classical music and write the film scene that the music could be used to score.
2. If you were to create a soundtrack of your life, what songs would you include? Why?

13

Sounds of the City

S OME PEOPLE LONG for the peace of the countryside, but others thrill to the beat of the city. Wherever you go, tune in to the sounds, and let them inform your writing.

In New York, the screech of the subway pulling into the station, steel on steel, the *whoosh* of airbrakes, and the ear-splitting blast of jackhammers can set my teeth on edge. But the Metropolitan Opera and the chatter of foreign languages that bounce me from neighborhood to neighborhood bring me pleasure. The din in Mumbai is legendary, with touters and hawkers at shop doors shouting, luring, accosting pass-ersby. I don my impassive look, my cloak of invisibility, and walk quickly, eyes straight ahead. There's no escaping tut-tut drivers who lean without stop on their beepy little horns, hoping to shoo motorbikes and cows from their path. But when I pass a temple and hear the harmonium and the chants, I feel grounded once again. In Paris, an accordionist in a park brings a smile to my face. In Rome, the church bells bong the hour and return me to the present.

When I gave the prompt "Sounds of the City" to one of my classes, we went coast to coast as people wrote for seven minutes. Each of the freewrites gave us a sense of time and place, beginning with this piece about New York City.

My cab tears through the Manhattan streets, a homing pigeon in search of an address. Another cab swings too close. *Honk*, they each burp a huge blast of noise, my driver mumbling in a language foreign to me. *His turban must be hot*, I think to myself. I roll my window down a little, and a mix of honking, braking, buses fuming, and who knows what sounds—the general hum of eight million people.

He drives up to my building and stops the cab. I open my door and cars squeeze by. A cyclist whizzes past and I think, "He's crazy." But he negotiates the cars and pedestrians. Young men in slacks and button-down shirts, ties loosened and sleeves rolled up, converse on cell phones, talking shop, or to a wife, a child. The voices of young women on their phones harmonize with the bass of men's. Dogs barking stop to look around. What do they think of the noise? A fire truck lumbers by, sirens squealing, the dogs' ears perk up. They hear it all, and what we miss.

In the same class, someone explored the sounds of Oakland, California:

When IBM agreed to anchor the revitalization of downtown Oakland, they moved the sales office into an island in the middle of what sometimes seemed to be a war zone. Perched ten stories above the street, we watched the metal dinosaurs loading containers at the dock and heard the occasional scuffles and shouts in the alley below. A shuttle bus rattled the two blocks between our guarded parking lot and the office, and bums would mutter a quick plea as they clutched their bottle-shaped paper bags and stumbled past. Farther afield, Chinatown meant the lilting tones of traders and customers, and the vibrant reds and yellows of apples and pears and more exotic fruits we didn't know how to name. We specialized in the five-dollar lunch, competing to find the best food—plates clattering and clashing behind a battered metal door—we could bolt down in our forty-five-minute break. BART rumbled and moaned underneath the street, escalators silently carrying us underground and off to meetings in San Francisco, where it was the click of high heels instead of the grind of construction equipment that reminded us we needed to be on our best behavior.

One writer, raised in San Francisco in the 1930s, added details of time and place:

> The man in the horse-drawn cart calls out in a loud sing-song voice, "Rags, bottles, sacks. Rags, bottles, sacks." I thought he was selling them, but Mother told me he was collecting them to sell.
> Of the mournful foghorns on the bay, a babysitter told me, "Those are the sounds of the dead wailing, because they can't find their way home."

Not every line in these freewrites is about sound, but the images and details that touch on the other senses add to the richness. In addition to lively verbs in the New York piece (*tears, burps, mumbles*), the cyclist whizzing by contributes to the chaos, the turbaned cabdriver helps us imagine a foreign language, and the dog that hears more than humans makes us realize that we're not even hearing all the sound. In the Oakland piece, images such as the "metal dinosaurs" loading containers at the dock and vibrant colors of Chinatown help us see the scenes. This writer covered a lot of territory in terms of sound—from buses rattling and bums muttering to plates clattering and high heels clicking. The lines about 1930s San Francisco, in the third example, take me to a place I would not know had the writer not shown it to me.

EXERCISE

Try writing using these prompts:

1. The Sounds of the City.
2. Go to a crowded noisy place, such as a food court at a busy mall. Sit and just listen for three minutes. Describe what you have heard. You may want to combine this with the dialogue exercise on page 77, but be sure to include ambient sounds.

14

Bird Talk

S WEET SONGBIRDS FLIT and warble on our hillside, their
songs sullied by caws of occasional crows. Some mornings
I want to shoo away the birds that squeak and scream, create
a pastoral wonderland where only birds that console are permitted in my orbit. Some days I want silence, no tweets or
twitters. *Stop that singing this minute!*

But nature is beyond my control. So I adjust my attitude
and enjoy the flits and calls.

When I asked a group of writers to tune in to their senses
while sitting outdoors, one imagined what the birds were saying with their "intermittent tweaks and caws—a world of organized adjustments we cannot know."

"This is my tree! My tree!"
"Yo! Where *are* you?"
"I'm over here! Over here!"
"I need a little help!"
"Where's the salad?"
"Worm! Worm!"

The writer shifts perspective from the birds' voices to her own
musings. Wherever her mind takes her pen, she is truly writing free, playful and poetic, braiding memory and imagination.

Do they even eat worms anymore? Have birds, like us, gone some whole other nutrition route? They *can't* be eating *worms* anymore. That's so passé.

What *are* the birds calling about? Might it not be *urgent* at all?

Might I be misreading the abruptness of their cries?

Maybe they're saying, "Ooh! Light wind under the left feather! Shimmering breath on the duck pond! Look!"

Maybe they are exclaiming about Love.

Maybe the birds are poets.

Maybe it isn't all practicality, like *we* think.

The birds have all gone quiet.

A distant dog.

The requisite summer hammering—the fixing of a gate.

Where are you?

Inhale. I remember.

EXERCISE

Find a place you enjoy outdoors, such as a forest, beach, park, or garden, where you can hear natural sounds. Bird calls, crashing waves, the crunch of pine needles as you walk, the squeak of a tree trunk rocking ever so slightly in the wind. Listen deeply and describe what you hear. What stories arise? If you live in a city where this isn't possible, write about *not* hearing the sounds of nature.

15

Voices without Words

FOR WEEKS I LAY ILL in Arezzo, Italy, staring at the
hotel-room ceiling. I couldn't walk, talk, or eat, but I
could listen. Through my open window I heard the voices of
the town. Though I barely spoke Italian beyond *ciao* and *pasta*,
I could tune in to the pitch, speed, and vibration of the voices.
Without deciphering the words, I could discern the speakers:
Franca, the owner of the hotel where I was staying; Dr. Tanzi,
who'd come to examine me after I realized my illness was serious; and his friend Gianni, who owned the antique store next
to the hotel.

I felt weak and delirious, but I knew I'd forget the details if
I didn't take notes while I was there. So one afternoon I pulled
myself together for fifteen minutes, sat up in bed, and jotted
down facts and impressions. Later, I thought about how to describe the voices without the usual adjectives.

Franca's voice is raspy deep, the ashtray at her desk in
the hotel lobby heaped with butts of Marlboros. I can
hear her chatting in the street as she crosses the Piazza
Grande to our hotel, her voice a slow whir and drone,
like a machine that's stuck, an army tank crawling over
rough terrain.

About the doctor I wrote:

Each evening at seven, the men of our neighborhood gather at the corner of the piazza, beneath my hotel window. Echoing on the cobblestones, I hear the basso profundo of *il dottore*, checking in with his friend Gianni.

I felt the comfort of deep male voices. The doctor's voice was a rumble; Gianni's, higher pitched in his throat. The dialogue took on a musical quality, a back-and-forth conversation, in which I assumed they caught up on their day.

Soaking in fever-twisted sheets, I struggled to find parallels in my suburban American life for these nightly reunions on the corner of the piazza.

I thought of the bar in my town back home, where I saw groups gather to drink and play pool after work. How much healthier this Italian version seemed!

I thought of friendships like my yoga group of three, which meets once a week at one of our homes. We've been together for more than ten years and fill each other in on everything that's "up" during sessions we've come to call "conversational yoga."

I thought of fellowships—meditation groups, religious institutions, book clubs—where people gather, tell the truth, and miss the regulars if they don't show up.

Yet there was something different about these connections with friends on the piazza, the one-on-one intimacy and reliable nightly check-ins.

At eight o'clock on the dot, the voices stilled. I heard footsteps on the cobblestones and imagined each man walking to his nearby apartment for dinner with his family.

After that I could only hear motorbikes gunning their engines at a nearby stop sign and the bells in the church tower signaling that another fifteen minutes had elapsed.

When you write, think about the voices of your characters,

from tone and pitch to speed and vibration. Someone who always whispers versus someone who overrides others in a loud, insistent tone. Someone with a stammer versus a silver-tongued baritone.

Closer to home, I've given the prompt "My Mother's Voice" for a freewrite. The results invariably reveal something about the writer's feelings about her mother. A few examples:

"Her voice was like the screech of power saw on steel."

"When she whispered good night, my mother's voice swaddled me in down."

Sometimes I wish I had tape recordings of people's voices, even in voicemail or on an old answering machine. It is hard to recollect the voice of my father, who's been gone more than twenty-five years.

EXERCISE

Use the following writing prompts:

1. My Mother's Voice.
2. My Father's Voice.
3. Select any character or person you'd like to write about Begin by describing the person's voice from the narrator's or another character's point of view. Segue into dialogue or a memory triggered by the voice. Go beyond describing the voice and let the story unfold.
4. Describe the tone of voice of a loved one who is deceased. Or write about your inability to hear it.

16

My Body Is My Instrument

WHAT INSTRUMENT DO you think I am?" I asked a composer who knew me well. I thought I was a cello, wide-hipped and voluptuous. But he said, "Violin."

I was flattered. A light and graceful instrument that had the range to move me. The number one instrument in my opinion.

Cellos are mellow. Low notes. Not me. And I'm certainly no second violin or viola. Definitely not brassy or reedy. And don't even think percussion.

When I was young I wanted to play the harp, be the harp, rippling sweet cascades of music. Now I think it's over-the-top angelic. I am not a harp.

I am a violin.

While I may not hit all the high notes and vibrato of my younger days, I am still well tuned, creating melodies playful and deep.

"What instrument do you think you are?" I asked my sister, who is a symphony conductor. "I can't answer that," she said. "I am the orchestra." Indeed, when I gave this prompt at a workshop, we nearly had an orchestra: strings, woodwinds, and drums.

Here's our impromptu ensemble:

A String

A string, not a wind
Zoning along the hair follicles in my ear

My father and his father played the viola
My granddaughter plays the violin
They're at the heart of my life
All is pulled away with each stroke of the bow
Elongated sound or pizzicato pluck
From me a memory of loss.
Left hand fretting and right hand flying.

Cello

Resonance, deep, low, continuo.
Bow drawn lovingly across the strings.
Fingers touch down, opening, sings.
Dvořák, Brahms, Bach.
There is no block
To love actually.

Clarinet

If I were an instrument, I would be a clarinet, accessible
but exotic, jazz and klezmer. I don't like to be the center
of attention, but like clarinets, I provide offbeat accom-
paniment and lovely harmony—with some stunning
opportunities to shine in the midst of the whole. I have
influence and authority but not the big, brassy voice of
the trumpet or the horns.

Drum

Like a woodpecker, *rat-a-tat-tat,* or a slow brush on the
hide of my skin. The *clack-clack* of a wooden drumstick
on the hard rim of my outsides. I rumble low, palms
down, like a heartbeat, *ba-boom, ba-boom, ba-boom.*
Sometimes jumping, seat out of the chair, feet moving,
with Creedence Clearwater or the Grateful Dead. A beat

to dance to. Heat up the fire, joy to the soul. I love the taiko drummers leaping and crashing, the sounds of the big drums, though I am more suited now to the smaller stage, the smaller circle, keeping a heartbeat, invitations to enter.

EXERCISE

Writing prompts:

- What instrument are you?
- What instrument would you like to be?

17

He Said, She Said

WRITERS DEVELOP THE ability to know when a line is a winner. As soon as you hear one, write it down. When I was shopping for saris in Mumbai, a salesman flung a rectangle of orange silk over his outstretched arm and exclaimed, "Madame, these are selling like a hotcake!" What a great lead for my story. *Thank you!* I thought. I left the shop and immediately jotted it down.

Even as I was having a conversation in a tourist office in southwest France, my writer's mind was observing, thinking: *This is classic.* I sensed the exchange would be an entertaining introduction to a piece that showed the challenge of my quest to learn more about foie gras, while conveying something about the Frenchman who was theoretically there to help me:

Lover of all things luxurious, I told the man at Sarlat's tourist office I wanted to learn more about foie gras.

"We have nothing in English." He turned to the next tourist in line.

"I can translate the French," I persisted.

"We have nothing in French. What do you want to know?"

"How is it made, what does it cost, how much is produced? Perhaps if I visited a farm where it is made . . . Would that be possible?"

"You could visit a farm and still you would know nothing," he sniffed.

Sometimes the power of dialect comes from the writer's ability to help us hear the accent or phrasing of the character. My grandmother lived in the United States for sixty years but never lost her Russian accent, and she garbled her grammar until the day she died. "I vant you should be be able . . . ," she attempted to conjugate the verb.

One student captured her Polish fitness trainer's accent when she wrote this dialogue:

"You have pretty good shape," says Jerzy, beginning his fine, forensic fitness analysis. "You don't have big, huge stomach or fat ass," he says, pointing to the projected photos. "You are well proportioned, but . . ." And that "but" seems to hang in the air forever. "You are fat all over. Even your neck is fat."

"Really? My neck?" I say as I tug at the flesh beneath my chin.

"Yes, even neck. But don't worry; we are going to change that," he says. Next he lays out the eating and exercise regimen I am supposed to follow during the next four months, the plan that promises to transform my body from "fat all over" to a lean, mean, hot mama machine.

Think how much tone of voice adds to the words that are spoken. How would you communicate that? You can do it with verbs, looks, or mannerisms. Usually in dialogue we keep it simple by using the verb "said" (or we eliminate the verb entirely if it's clear we're going back and forth between two characters), but when I wrote that the man in the Sarlat tourist office "sniffed," I implied his attitude. If a character hunches his shoulders with palms up when he speaks, that gives us information and a visual image.

EXERCISE

Here's a dialogue exercise you can do with a partner. Each of you decides what character to be, but you don't tell each other. You might be a teenage male who's the member of a youth gang, a deacon at the church, an addled geriatric, or a shopaholic. You can think up a fictional character or base it on someone you know.

Pass a piece of paper back and forth, each writing a sentence or two in character, creating a dialogue between you. At the end, try to guess who your partner's character was.

Here is another dialogue exercise. Going someplace you don't usually go may help you tune in to what's actually being said. It might be a biker bar, an ethnic neighborhood, or a gospel church. Eavesdrop, listen, take notes. This will train you to tune in to interesting dialogue. No mundane conversations like, "Hi, how are you?" "Fine. How are you?" Wait two to four weeks, then write a piece describing that place, including dialogue. With hindsight, are there details you wish you had noted?

You're likely to find more action and "sound bites" in places where people are not expected to be quiet. Still, even at the main branch of the San Francisco Public Library, I've found good material, as I sat across the table from a homeless man.

18

Chants Encounter

C HANTING IS A WAY to settle our minds and connect with a spiritual path that calls to us through memory or choice. We may not know what the words mean, but the rhythms can evoke memories from our lives or even memories that seem to reach back before our time. That settling in and recall can lead to deep and powerful writing. Sometimes a chant is new to us, but the repetition stops our mental chatter, makes our heads and bodies vibrate, and takes us beyond logical thinking.

"R-r-reem, r-r-reem." The guru from India trilled the *r*, letting the "eem" fade away like a gong, dissipating from sound to silence.

"This mantra usually works," he said.

In my mind, I tried it with different vowels: *R-r-ram, r-r-rim, r-r-rem, r-r-room.*

The "reem" reverberated high in my nasal cavity, resounding like a bell. I felt calmed by the bell, the gong.

A cowbell from India hung from my kitchen cabinet door. When I passed it, I swung the rough-hewn wooden clapper against the copper. How could such a humble stick make such a rich, sweet sound? It was the perfect note to bring me back to center.

My friend's three-year-old daughter gonged it incessantly on her visits. I took it down so the adults could converse.

"I like that bell," she told me.

"It's from India," I replied.

"Oh, I love India," she said. She'd never heard of the country before. Maybe someday we'll go there together.

In the meantime, I chant my mantra silently twice a day, before meals when possible, as advised. The resonance of the sound grounds me. When I catch my mind wandering, I pull it gently back to "R-r-reem."

A few months later, when I was leading a workshop at Green Gulch Farm and Retreat Center in Northern California, we chanted aloud. A Buddhist chant with a percussive beat. Not knowing what the words meant allowed me to lose myself in the rhythm, feel the vibrations in my body. Focusing on the words of the chant left no room in my mind for wandering. No room for thought. What a relief!

As soon as we stopped chanting we picked up our pens to write. I could still feel the vibration in my hands, my chest, my head. And the syncobeat, the rhythm of my heart. My mind cleared, my body pulsed. I felt grounded.

One chanter wrote:

Resonance, trust it.
Hand on chest
Sound of the heart.
Ears awake
Sit still.

Here are two chants you can try. Don't worry about the melodies or rhythms. For five minutes, just hear what comes out of your mouth and pay attention to the vibrations in your head and body.

The first is a simple Hindu chant: "*Om shanti, om shanti, om shanti om.*" (*Shanti* means "peace.")

The second is part of the Buddhist chant we used in the writing exercise at our Green Gulch workshop.

Kan zee own
Na mu Butsu
Yo Butsu u in
Yo Butsu u en
Bup po so en
Jo raku ga jo
Cho nen Kan zee own
Bo nen Kan zee own
Nen nen ju shin ki
Nen nen fu ri shin

EXERCISE

Choose a chant from any spiritual path that calls to you, and repeat it over and over. If you chant out loud, you're more likely to feel the vibrations in your head and body. After five minutes of chanting, write using one of these prompts:

- "I'll never forget . . ."
- "The most important thing . . ."

19

At Water's Edge

THE GRAVEL PATH crunches as I walk alongside Lake
Como to the Villa Melzi. My senses alert, I feel the texture of the pebbles beneath my feet and listen to the crackling
sound. I know these perceptions will find their way into my
writing.

The lake laps gently, a soothing sound, like breath.

*If there were a bench, I would sit here and bask in this sound, I
say to myself*

Eccola! A bench. Most of the benches that line the lake are
slatted wood, painted green, with backs like park benches,
but this one is unlike the others—modern, sleek and backless,
smooth white stone.

In late October, the end of the tourist season, the park is
quiet. Japanese maples burn red and orange. The sycamores
are bare.

Wavelets with glassy rounded tops rise six inches, then flutter with happy, white-bubbled edges, rippling to the shore.

After sunset, the lake is black silk, rippling ever so slightly.
Back at the hotel, from my balcony I watch a car ferry glide
seamlessly from Bellagio bound for Menaggio. It seems to be
pulled across the surface by a taut and invisible rope.

"I feel so calm when I remember that lake," I tell a friend
months later.

"Just read your words and you'll be there," she says.

While ocean waves crash, break, and roar, we often describe lakes with gentle words. They lap and whoosh, leaving soft, frilly foam that percolates and disappears.

At a beach in Santa Cruz, our group of writers sat on the edge of the ocean, the edge of the world. I offered two prompts: "The ocean helps me remember . . ." and "On the edge of the ocean . . ." Much of the writing was poetic as we listened to the ocean's rhythmic rushing sound, "even though it's not rushing," as one person wrote, adding, "I took a picture with my senses."

I love living on a coast with three thousand miles of continent to ground me. I thought about how the ocean symbolizes freedom and new frontiers, about my grandparents who all crossed oceans (Atlantic or Pacific) to "make it" in America. I thought of my mother, who loves to travel and passed that love on to her children. In my freewrite I considered the double-edged sword of travel: going toward something new or running away. I realized that I have shifted from my passion for the ocean to a calmer love of lakes.

> On the edge of the ocean, the edge of the world. The ocean makes me remember my love of places far away. Lands unknown and known to which I long to return.
>
> Just get me away from *here*, wherever *here* is—my daily life of routine and obligations.
>
> Travel gives me perspective.
>
> I used to be a beach person. Now I am drawn to lakes. More serene. I'm calmed by the gentle, rhythmic *whoosh* of water scampering shallow toward the sand, foamy, lacy white.
>
> Ocean waves, on the other hand, crash and roar. In the distance, the water swells into a hill, a wave, folds

over itself, and breaks. How can water break? Break-water, water break. Like the water, water like. Hey, I am like Gertrude Stein, a cubist with words.

The ocean makes me remember that I am not in control. I cannot stop the ebb and flow. The currents, the tides, the rise and fall.

The ocean makes me remember that I am a tiny speck, a grain of sand. No. Less than a grain of sand.

The ocean makes me remember, air can be fresh and clean, faintly smelling of salt.

Yesterday, I thought the sound of the ocean was relentless. Turn down the volume! The ocean has the last laugh. An endless bubble and churn.

Like the piece of tin in a radio sound-effects booth—fake thunder and rumble, with a touch of gravel in its throat. Pebbles rattling in the roar.

In just fifteen minutes I feel sunburned. The delicate skin on the tops of my feet, the sturdier skin on my forearms, weathered more on the left than the right from a lifetime of being in the driver's seat.

Note that I repeat (incorrectly) the prompt "The ocean makes me remember" several times. This repetition is a good technique when you run out of things to say. It gives you a fresh start and impels you forward. The ideas don't have to be connected.

One writer began with the prompt, then veered off to a memory of the Caribbean, full of energy and color.

At the edge of the ocean I remember a dream of oceans, of the many and the one I'd like to return to, the ocean I look for in all others: the one where I'm on a sail-boat, about five years old, cutting across an expanse of iridescent blue green scattered with golden sparkles. It's the Caribbean, land of the exotic, of lizards, palms, and pink houses, and mostly of this—this wild greenish blue water going on in all directions, split apart by the prow of the boat. A woman lends me a sun hat with a red tie beneath it. I tie it under my chin, we pull up onto a sandy island, I get out, I swim. The water is different from the ocean around Long Island Sound: it has the sweetness of mango and papaya, it mixes cool and warm like a tropical night, but most of all it has that particular wash of colors, the brilliant tropical aquamarine turning sandy beige where the bottom rises toward the surface. This is my first experience of absolute intoxication. Nothing rivals it, not even the first time I went to see *The Nutcracker* at Lincoln Center, when I cried at the end of the show because it was so beautiful I wanted to watch it all over again, right then and there. This is as transporting as the ballet *and* it keeps on going, no curtain falling, no exiting the theater. It keeps on going hour after hour and day after day until I come down with chicken pox and am grounded in our motel room, taking oatmeal baths. Outside the window I can see the weather has changed, the water a dark green, now, with whitecaps. My father has gone to the rock pier to fish. A horse eats grass in a meadow near the beach. I stand inside holding my bunny rabbit, wondering when I'll be well enough to go swimming again.

So many sensory images and details bring this piece alive, as well as the rhythm of the words. The color of the water and the sweetness of the fruit. From her dream of oceans as the freewrite begins, we are brought back to earth by concrete images: a little girl stilled by chicken pox and oatmeal baths, holding her bunny rabbit, looking out the window.

The writer has created a satisfying "tie-back" ending, simply by letting the words flow. She has returned full circle to the water, wondering when she will swim again.

Notice that beyond images and details, each of these free-writes about lakes and oceans creates a feeling—the calm of Lake Como, the roughness of the ocean, the sensuality of the Caribbean. It has been said that we remember little of what people say or do. What we remember is how they made us feel. The same is true of writing. We may not remember specific words, but we remember how we felt when reading or listening to a story or poem.

EXERCISE

As a prompt, start with this opening line: "The ocean helps me remember . . ."

20

The Sound of Silence

S ILENCE. STILLNESS. SOLITUDE. These are great topics for writing. Tune in to the absence of sound. How is it different from everyday life? Is silence really silent?

Sometimes life reminds me of the Zen story where a horse is galloping down the road; its rider seems to be on an urgent mission. As they race past, a bystander calls out, "Where are you going?" "I don't know!" the rider yells back. "Ask the horse."

I've often slowed down by going to places that invite a more leisurely pace—Ayurvedic spas in India, jungle temples in Bali, or lakes in northern Italy.

Recently I looked closer to home and discovered I could go deep without going far. I went on a three-day retreat at a monastery overlooking Big Sur, where the monks encourage quiet contemplation. I didn't speak to other retreatants; instead we communicated with smiles and silent greetings. I found the sound of silence and I did daily freewrites about my experience.

It is a relief to be free of small talk. No "Where are you from?" and "What do you do?" No labels based on credentials.

But even the silence is not silent. Birds cry, the wind rustles dry autumn leaves, the gravel crunches as we walk to the kitchen to collect our noon meal, which we bring back to our rooms to eat in solitude.

Like a vacation, this getaway gave me perspective—a chance to step out of my everyday life. But it was different: no architectural wonders, no must-see sights, no Michelin-starred restaurants.

My inner gyroscope searches for center, and I wonder how I will fill the day without the busyness of work, my exercise routine, or social life.

But I noticed that when I awoke, I didn't feel like a racehorse at the starting gate, galloping mentally through deadlines, duties, and demands. I could let the day unfold. Time is passing effortlessly with walks and hikes, yoga, meditation, reading, and writing. I would happily stay here longer.

Back home, I made small changes that had big effects. I am willing to show up for my writing, and when possible I do it first, before the day's other tasks that clamor for priority. Silence helps me pay attention, and I have tools to clear the mental chatter, so that I can access my best work. For example, I limit my daily e-mail and voicemail check-ins. I meditate each morning. No matter how busy I am, exercise is non-negotiable, for—as I mention throughout this book—some of my best writing ideas come while I am meditating, walking, or swimming. And these are not merely the results of sorting through and reorganizing the same few options my logical computer brain is aware of. Rather, an entirely new idea often comes to me in a moment of inspiration. My job is to be prepared to receive it.

It's not that I became perfectly serene, but I have a better idea of how to find balance. At least for now, I'm riding the horse, not the other way around.

One of my students wrote about silence when she was on her own writing retreat:

Silence is a large man, with a huge Buddha smile.

Silence is the great Protector, the holder of all things.
Silence is a Father. He creates a place.
He lies down on his back and lets us play on his
   stomach, climbing up his knees, sliding down again.
With large hands prepared to catch us if we fall.
And catching me, he sets me down gently, bowing
As if I were his partner and we had just shared great
   intimacy.
For we do.

He brings me cool glasses of lemonade in the midst of
   hot, rush-hour traffic
When I've forgotten how the air-conditioning works in
   my car—
I am that agitated, that frightened.
"Here," he says, smiling his large smile.

Silence is darkness; at times I am lost under his armpit,
   among the soft folds of his shirt, and I don't know it.
I batter at it, but it does not hit back. It waits.
Until I see the folds, undo them, come out from under
   and onto his forearm, say, or chest—and again, he
   smiles, holding me.

Silence says, "I am" in that God-shaking-the-earth way,
   then laughs,
and holds *all* of us, of It, in a great, vast smile.

EXERCISE
────────────

Sit in a relaxed position in silence for ten minutes. Then write
what being in silence taught you.

PART THREE

Smell

TAKE A WHIFF OF Vicks VapoRub and suddenly you're writing about that winter night when your mother tenderly applied a compress to your four-year-old chest. Inhale fresh lavender and you're transported to the outdoor market in Arles, writing about sachets in your lingerie drawer that, fifteen years later, still smell of Provence.

We see when there is light, taste when something crosses our tongue, hear when sounds are audible. But we smell with every breath.

Smell bypasses thought, jumping from the cerebral cortex straight to the limbic system, an ancient section of our brain. It can snap us to another time and place, and excavate memories and emotions long forgotten.

Smell has been called the mute sense because scents are often difficult to describe. We use similes ("the baby smelled like caramel"), or rely on the fact that others have smelled what we describe. Sometimes we resort to vague descriptions of how smells make us feel: It smells repulsive; it smells delightful. While we perceive subtle gradations of color (fire-engine red, crimson, rose), we don't have such fine-tuning for smell.

As a writer I'm aware that the sense of smell is underused, so I try to pay attention. On my walks, I revel in the sharp, heady scent of eucalyptus. At the hardware store I sniff the mothballs and cedar. In Paris and Florence perfumeries, I sort through sweet florals and earthy musks.

Strolling through North Beach, the Little Italy of San Francisco, I think, *What does coffee smell like?* Well, it smells like . . . coffee. Then a friend hands me a raw coffee bean, and it has no smell at all. It's the roasting that brings out the scent we call coffee.

Just say *caramelized onions* or *raw garlic,* and most of us know the smell. We begin to salivate if it's something we like to eat. Smell is often connected to taste. When Molly Birnbaum, an aspiring chef, lost her sense of smell after an accident, she said that bread was like a grainy sponge and coffee was merely bitter heat. Much like the way we feel when we have a cold and experience textures, not tastes.

For those who haven't lost this sense, coffee may smell bitter or acrid; garlic, sharp or pungent. But what does that really smell like? Is there a simile that would convey the scent in a fresh way? "The garlic smelled like razor-sharp knives." "The stewed cabbage smelled like rotten breath." It may be challenging to describe a smell—roses and jasmine, baby powder or Play-Doh, fresh ink on a printed page—but rise to meet the challenge.

If you were deprived of your other senses, would your sense of smell become keener? Helen Keller, who lost her sight and ability to hear at the age of nineteen months, was so attuned to smells that she could tell a thunderstorm was approaching by the odor coming up from the earth. Her early lessons with her teacher Annie Sullivan were filled with the "breath of the woods—the fine, resinous odor of pine needles, blended with the perfume of wild grapes."

21

Rose in Bloom

WE WERE SITTING in a rose garden in May, surrounded by sweet and heady old-timey roses that hadn't had the fragrance bred out of them. Smell is often described by using senses other than smell. Here one writer relies on touch and sound to convey the scent of a rose. As this freewrite reveals, writing from the senses allows us to explore the ineffable, intangible, intuitive places, where we *know* certain things are true without concrete evidence.

The best thing about rose smell is that you *feel* it against your skin.

The roses smell so soft, like the lightest, softest touch.

Saying, "See? This is *allowed*. This kind of gentle? Happens."

Every day. Gentle and subtle, like no one knows it's there, but it is. That's the world.

Shhhhh. Smell.

Gentle. Like a pause.

Like rain.

If you could hear one raindrop, that would be the smell of the rose.

Your touch on my cheek.

Ooh, you mean that's Allowed?

You mean we get to be like we *are*?

Quiet, almost invisible. But—not—

But No—even if we *were* invisible, we are Here.

Smell? Can you smell that?

Even the word "smell" is too harsh for what you're doing when you smell a rose. Inhale, gently, sweetly, slowly, like petting a rabbit and it doesn't run away. A touch so gentle—

God's touch must be like that. Like this.

Oh the smell, the scent, the hot stones, the sweat-shirt, the peach-colored petals.

Your hands, fingers, really—gently cupping my head as we stood together.

And I remember—ohhh, it can be like this.

Shhhh. Smell.

This writer found a way to convey the ineffable fragrance of roses. Some floral scents are easier to describe than others. After my sister visited the spring iris show in Florence, she surprised me with this information: "Purple irises smell like grapes; pale orange, like apricots; yellow, like lemons. Some colors are harder to describe: burgundy like a dusky mystery; white like clean, fresh laundry."

EXERCISE

Come up with five similes to describe smells. Here are a few to get you started: coffee (smells like . . .), scallions, dirty socks, wet wool mittens, honeysuckle.

22

Three-Note Harmony

I N HER WONDERFUL BOOK *A Natural History of the Senses,*
Diane Ackerman writes about a visit to International Flavors and Fragrances Inc. in New York City, home to "the best
noses in the business." Combining flowers, roots, animal secre-
tions, grasses, oils, and artificial smells to create new scents,
one perfumer says her work is similar to composing music.
There are simple fragrances made from two or three ingredients, much like a two- or three-piece band. At the other end
of the spectrum are complex perfumes made up of multiple
notes and tones, more like a large orchestra. But whatever the
fragrance, the notes must be in harmony and balance. Several
layers may come through, but if any is too strong, the scent
will not be well accepted.

Chanel No. 5, a classic scent created in the 1920s, is an example of a well-balanced perfume whose combination of top,
middle, and base notes appealed to the noses of the market-
place. First you smell the top note, an aldehyde (a synthetic
scent based on those found in nature). Then, you inhale the
middle notes of jasmine, rose, lily of the valley, orris, and
ylang-ylang. Next you sense the base notes, which cause the
perfume to linger: vetiver, sandalwood, cedar, vanilla, amber,
civet, and musk. Base notes, Ackerman tells us, are almost always of animal origin, "ancient emissaries of smell that transport us across the woodlands and savannas."

Smells fall into basic categories, almost like primary colors, says Ackerman: minty, floral, ethereal (such as pears), musky, resinous (such as camphor), foul (rotten eggs), and acrid (vinegar). Obviously, not all of these find their way into perfumes. Knowing the language of smell helps us write in a way that conveys the fragrances. But for more vivid writing, go beyond these categories and come up with specific scents or similes: "She had the subtle fragrance of a ripe and wide-hipped Anjou pear."

I recall a long-ago trip to Paris, where experts at a *parfumerie* chose the fragrance that was "me." How annoyed I was that they selected spicy, woodsy scents instead of roses, jasmine, or other symbols of frilly, feminine allure! I ignored them and bought Madame Rochas and Joy. I was only twenty-one, drawn to notes of the sweetest blossoms. Today, musky, earthy fragrances have complexity, depth, and mystery that draw me in.

EXERCISE

Would you choose a sweet, floral scent for yourself or one that is spicy and woodsy? How would you describe it? If another fragrance is "you," how would you describe the scent?

23

Cleopatra Isn't Welcome Here

C LEOPATRA'S SHIP HAD perfumed sails. Incense burners surrounded her throne, and she was scented from head to toe with oil of roses and violets, almond and honey.

Here, where I live in Marin County, California, she would be a social outcast because so many places are fragrance-free zones.

Not in terms of nature—the woods are alive with the fresh menthol scent of eucalyptus and the spicy fragrance of pine. Gardens sing with rosemary and lavender, roses and star jasmine. But when it comes to man-made smells, there are a lot of imaginary red circles with diagonal slashes through them. Signs posted in conference rooms ask us to refrain from using scented lotions and shampoos. In some places we are forbidden from wearing clothes washed in detergents that are not fragrance-free.

I am not unsympathetic. When a man or woman doused in cologne sits near me in a movie theater, I am forced to change my seat. I wouldn't be able to concentrate on the film with the uninvited odor invading my space. Choosing not to sit for hours inhaling someone else's perfume is like choosing not to listen to loud solo cell phone conversations or certain kinds of music. It's a sensory choice like not watching films that disturb, or choosing hot showers, not cold.

Like Cleopatra, I'd like to control my environment. Only let in scents that make me feel good, such as lavender and rose, and ban those I find unpleasant—think stinky socks or a room filled with blooming narcissus.

But to cleanse my environment of smells, even those I don't relish, shuts a door on memory and imagination, critical tools for writing more deeply. The scent of pastry in the oven can take you back to the day your grandmother taught you to bake your first apple pie. The smell of dirty feet can remind you what it was like to raise your sons. Smell is a sense worth keeping around.

In classes, sometimes I use scents as prompts. I might hand out sprigs of rosemary or lavender, or give each person a small container of Vicks VapoRub or cedar chips. (I give everyone the same thing to smell.)

When I used cedar balls as a prompt, the freewrites covered a wide range of topics. Two people wrote about hope chests, pointing to what the chests symbolized in their eras.

> My mother's cedar chest is in my basement. In her day it was called a hope chest—this was obviously before Helen Gurley Brown and Gloria Steinem. Hope what? Just go and get laid and the rest will take care of itself. But I digress. Since my mother has been dead for seven years, the cedar in this chest is no longer about hope, now it's more of an embalming fluid.
>
> This fall I intend to, that is I hope to, unpack both her chest and her effect on my life. Like the dusty reddish box, I have kept the memory of her transgressions against me in pristine condition, locked away in my emotions. It's time to unpack her stuff both downstairs and deep within me.

In the next example, the writer tells us of life without a hope chest:

The sweet pungent smell of cedar balls wafts from my cousin's long wooden hope chest. I peer inside and take in the hand-embroidered pillowcases, the crisp white sheets, some towels peeking out like little tufts of hair. I want a hope chest. This is what little girls dream of in 1958. We collect items that will start our homes with a husband, once we marry.

The thought that a perfumed hope chest would not exist doesn't enter my mind, but it never comes to be. My parents can't afford to buy the glossy piece of furniture, so I put the pillowcases my grandma embroidered for me in a drawer to live out their lonely lives, never feeling the soft hair of my husband, who existed in my mind.

Didn't every young girl think she would marry? Is that what the hope chest meant?

When a student, whose parents were Holocaust survivors, heard this "hope chest" freewrite, she marveled at the idea. "That would never occur in my family!" she exclaimed.

"No," I replied. "Some families have 'hopeless chests.'"

Her freewrite, triggered by the scent of cedar, was about mildew and old age.

I can't stand the musty, damp mildew smell of old homes. Perhaps because my father said they were haunted with ghosts. Or maybe the problem is in my head. Literally, not mentally, in the orifice attached, the nasal column structured too small. It's my nose, a leftover from a Roman time or perhaps the beak of an elder Jew wandering around the desert dust for too long. Maybe my nasal cavity is just too small and smells are too strong and the superstition of ghosts makes the situation more dramatic than necessary. No matter. There are things I don't like, including oldness in any form.

EXERCISE

Use the following writing prompts:

1. Inhale the scent of cedar chips or mothballs. How would you describe the smell? What story comes to mind?
2. Describe the smell of a compost heap or a horse stable.
3. Tell me what it's like to walk the gauntlet of smokers huddled outside an office building during their cigarette break.
4. On the sweeter side, take a whiff of lavender or smell a peppermint tea bag. Write whatever comes up.

24

Odors of Time and Place

LIFE IS A SOUP OF SMELLS, some lovely as a rose in the garden or cookies in the oven, some stinky as a baby's diaper. In New York City, I'm assaulted by fumes from the exhaust pipe of a bus or stale urine in the stairwell of an underground garage, where I hold my breath to walk down to my car. On the other hand, a whiff of basil when the door swings open at a Thai restaurant can be alluring. The fragrance of tomato sauce and crispy crust from Ray's Pizza on 59th Street makes me crave a slice.

Fragrance and *aroma* connote more pleasant smells; *scent* can go either way; *stench* shifts us to the nasty end of the continuum.

While I'd rather write about smells that please, the other side of lovely can catapult us into scenes we relate to, even if we've never been there.

In his novel *Perfume*, Patrick Süskind describes the stench of eighteenth-century Paris, from the stink of manure and urine in the streets to the smell of rotten cabbage and mutton fat. He points to caustic lyes and skins in the tanneries and congealed blood in the slaughterhouses, then turns to the stench of the people smelling of sweat and unwashed clothes, rotting teeth, and onion breath.

I like to surround myself with roses, cashmere, and classical music, so you can imagine my reluctance to hike to the compost heap at Green Gulch Farm. But experiencing a sensation helps me write about it, and I wanted to write about an unpleasant smell. Walking down the road, past furrowed fields that lay fallow in winter, I arrived at the compost field—a moonscape with fifteen piles, each about ten feet in diameter, most covered with blue plastic tarps, their corners weighted down with tires. They were marked by three-foot wooden signs, instructing people not to mix and mingle waste: BRUSH LESS THAN ½ DIAMETER—NO INVASIVES, BLACKBERRIES OK. WARM COMPOST—MANURE. WARM COMPOST—NO MANURE. *So tidy and well organized*, I thought.

Stepping around horse droppings and mud puddles warming in the sun, I bent over one of the compost piles and didn't smell a thing. *Even their garbage doesn't smell.* I wondered about Buddhist baby diapers. Then the breeze shifted and brought me a sour whiff. Later I learned that healthy compost doesn't necessarily smell bad. The putrid odor may result from a heap getting too wet, as it had that day after a storm.

Nature, I remembered once again, is more than frankincense and myrrh. It is armpits and burning hair and spinach abandoned in the vegetable hydrator, turning into soppy green goop. It is feet, damp and riddled with fungus, and it is warm compost, with and without manure.

Heat releases odors as the molecules move. In *State of Wonder,* Ann Patchett writes about India:

There is a heat of the day to contend with and then the heat of so many bodies, their sweat and perfume, the sharp scent of spice carried in the smoke of vendors' fires and the bitter smell of marigolds strung into garlands.

I smell the bodies, the smoke and the specific scent of the marigolds. In another chapter, she describes a character in the Amazon jungle:

The minute she stepped into the musty wind of the tropical air-conditioning, Marin smelled her own wooliness. She pulled off her light spring coat and then the zippered cardigan beneath it, stuffing them into her carry-on where they did not begin to fit, while every insect in the Amazon lifted its head from the leaf it was masticating and turned a slender antenna in her direction. She was a snack plate, a buffet line, a woman dressed for springtime in the North.

What a wonderful image: every insect lifting its head and spinning toward this human snack plate.

EXERCISE

1. Write about an unpleasant odor.
2. Write about a scent that pleases you.

25

Scents of the Season

I MAGINE YOU'RE AT a Thanksgiving dinner where you can see the food but smell none of the aromas. The colors are important—the crimson cranberry relish, the autumnal orange yams. But the vision seems bare when compared to the feelings evoked by the fragrance of a traditional Thanksgiving meal. The smell of crisp-cooked turkey skin, a thin layer of fat saturating the tender and savory breast and leg mingles with the slightly acrid aroma of Brussels sprouts. Rosemary and sage flavor the stuffing, sugar sparkles on the piecrust. The cranberry relish is sugary sweet and spicy tart with orange zest. The mashed potatoes are buttery, salty, mild, or savory. Nutmeg, cinnamon, and cloves turn apple cider or red wine into a festive treat.

If I'm in California on Thanksgiving Day, I often walk through Blithedale Canyon, along the dry creeks, before the rainy season has begun. The air is thick, gray, still. Amber lights warm the interiors of old cedar-shingled homes that sit expectant, waiting for guests to arrive for late-afternoon dinner. I breathe in deeply the spicy scent of Monterey pine and cedar.

A five-year-old boy is gathering pine cones and cotoneaster boughs rich with clusters of bright orange berries. His mother tosses a stick for their golden retriever. "Look, Simon," she calls to her son, "this piece of wood is like a sculpture. We can use it as part of the centerpiece with the pine cones and berries."

The front door of the next house I pass bursts open as the owner rushes out, smiling, to her car to bring in the wine and sparkling water. The sweet golden scent of roasting turkey makes my muscles melt with memory.

When I'm in New York, we drive out to my brother's house on Long Island for a meal that none can rival. We enter through the back door of his home and pass through the kitchen, warm with late-afternoon winter light. Here, the air is thick with mouth-watering smells.

I'm a traditionalist when it comes to this meal, although we long ago abandoned the gelatinous cranberry sauce that plopped onto the plate in the shape of the can that housed it. But one year my brother, a creative cook, decided to make turducken—a deboned chicken, within a deboned duck, within a deboned turkey. Between each bird was a layer of homemade stuffing, some with Andouille sausage imported from New Orleans. The birds were sliced on an angle to reveal the layers like an archaeological dig. A beautiful presentation. Now give me that old-fashioned golden roasted turkey, please, and pass the savory stuffing.

When I think of my brother's house on those late November afternoons, I feel the warmth of escaping the outdoor chill. I remember the toasty comfort of being together and the kitchen aromas that say family and friends have gathered and will eat until they can eat no more.

EXERCISE

1. Take a walk in your neighborhood. As you walk, write down words or phrases of things you pass that relate to the senses.
2. Write about the scents of Thanksgiving. Describe the

smells emanating from the kitchen before the meal and the smells of the actual dishes when served. "Family Dinner" is always a great prompt, and a holiday meal may evoke memories from "warm gathering" to "you won't believe what happened."

26

Bridging Smell and Taste

TASTE MAY BE SWEET or acrid, but it's always influenced by smell, the connection of nose and tongue. When we think of taste, we are incorporating smell, whether we realize it or not, and we often refer to taste when describing smell. Wine is made solely from grapes, for example, yet because of the aromas they release, we use many words that call up other tastes, like black currants, pepper, and smoke.

Zeroing in on this smell-taste connection and on the emotional content of smell, chefs such as Grant Achatz create dishes that trigger intense memories and emotional reactions.

At his restaurant, Alinea, in Chicago, Achatz and his colleagues have discovered clever ways to deliver aroma as part of a dish. For example, for one item they fill small plastic pillows (covered in handmade linen sleeves to hide the plastic) with air scented with orange rind, lavender, nutmeg, or any other fragrance that might enhance a particular dining experience. The plate is presented upon the bag, which is pierced with a syringe to release the smell just before serving.

For another entrée, they create the aroma of spring by placing a small serving bowl of poached turbot directly on top of a hyacinth, which they've set in a larger serving bowl. Servers release the floral scent at the table by pouring hot water over the outer bowl.

For me, the pièce de résistance is the pheasant dish that

evokes another season, autumn, when served with narrow oak twigs, the leaves still smoldering after being torched in the kitchen.

I don't pour boiling water over flowers or set leaves on fire in my writing workshops, but I do use kitchen smells to prompt writing. In one class, I asked students to inhale garlic that I had crushed, then to write whatever came up.

Two students of Italian descent had strong responses to the scent of garlic. One student recalled her writing retreat with me in Tuscany.

Ahh, garlic—the essence of Italy! Walking the narrow medieval streets of Arezzo in the early afternoon, I smell meals being prepared by the *nonne* for their families. I hear three generations—from *nonni* to *nipoti*—arriving for lunch, the air permeated by the smell of garlic simmering in olive oil.

Eating in quaint restaurants, immersed in the essence of garlic, my senses revel, but my gut rebels. Relegated to my tiny Italian apartment, I cook rice, veggies, and chicken with no garlic or olive oil. My taste buds mourn.

The second student writes in a different tone, reflecting her "hold nothing back" personality.

Garlic, *aglio*, has become so acceptable in America—kind of like gay marriage. When I was a little kid, in the last century, and living in Watsonville, which is to say, nowhere, garlic was held in ill repute, almost as bad as the ladies of the same phrase. Garlic was ethnic. It made your breath smell. It wasn't American.

In my house we knew better. We were eating gnocchi with pesto alla Genovese, reeking with garlic, and pasta with my mother's *sugo* built upon a base of garlic and onions. At our kitchen table we sneered as we thought of those poor American *bastardi* eating chipped beef on toast or potpies or whatever bland, miserable food they ate.

I never wanted to join the American way of eating, and I never dreamed they would adopt ours. Maybe they just smelled our garlic-laced Italian cooking over the back fences of America. I don't have any idea how the country converted.

I liked it better the other way, when only we knew the secrets of eating excellence. Actually, they think they know more than they really do—I see pesto made with very little garlic and canola oil as an ingredient and I say, "*Porca miseria.*"

Sometimes we write to sort out our feelings, but both these writers are grounded and clear. They know how to do free-writes on the spot, fast and spontaneous, without editing. Neither is afraid to reveal the truth or explore wherever the writing takes her.

EXERCISE

Use the following prompts:

1. Crush a clove of garlic, inhale the scent, and write a memory or scene.
2. Choose a season and write about the smells that evoke that time of year for you.
3. Smell a sprig of rosemary, lavender, or any other herb, and write what comes to mind.

PART FOUR

Taste

E ATING CONSCIOUSLY centers us in the moment and en-
hances our daily lives with the sensual pleasures of taste
sensations and textures.

The five basic tastes—sweet, bitter, sour, salty, umami—
result from a chemical reaction between stimuli (food) in the
mouth reacting with receptors (taste buds).

Sweetness, which most people find pleasurable, is produced by the presence of sugars. It can come straight from
the tree, like crunchy fresh apples (of so many varieties, from
sweet to tart), or may be baked with sugar to bubbling sweetness in an apple pie.

Bitterness, sometimes perceived as sharp or unpleasant,
is found in drinks like coffee and tonic water (quinine) and
foods like citrus peel and unsweetened cocoa, as well as certain greens, such as dandelion, chicory, and escarole.

Sourness is the taste that detects acidity, as in vinegar. Salt-
iness is produced primarily by the presence of sodium ions,
found in foods from lox to potato chips.

Umami is a Japanese word referring to a savory, pungent,
meaty taste. While it seems to defy definition, umami is often
translated as "deliciousness" or "essence," and is characteris-
tic of cheese, soy sauce, and many Asian foods. Some call it
"the other pleasant taste," along with sweetness.

You'll see references to some of these tastes in the chapters
that follow. You'll also find a vocabulary for writing about taste

and taking descriptions of food beyond "delicious." You'll see how writing about the smell, texture, and sound of food can help us taste it, and how adding one ingredient at a time to a dish changes the taste. Above all, you'll discover how particular foods open up doors to memory, story, and imagination.

While many chapters in this section involve food, taste is a broader topic. Think what it's like to lick your lover's skin, chew a blade of summer grass, or taste the salty ocean air. Sense what it's like to bite down on a piece of aluminum foil. Not exactly a taste, but a sensation we can imagine, even if we've never experienced it.

27

Cooking Lessons

NOURISHMENT IS ABOUT so much more than the nutri-
ents we find in food. It is about the farmers who produced it, the people with whom we share our meals, and those
who taught us how to cook. It may make you ask, "Whom do I
consider family?" and gives us another perspective for thinking about relationships.

My mother didn't teach me how to cook. Instead she
taught me to aim for the top, grab the brass ring—"though
gold would be nice." She schooled me in the Three Ps of Success: be Persistent and a little bit Pushy; Patience is overrated.

After I graduated from law school, Mom continued to
prompt my success during our telephone check-ins. "When
are you getting married? You won't have your looks forever." She was just being honest. "When was your last Weight
Watchers meeting?" She considered this a neutral question.
Her helpful admonitions followed me across the country,
from New York to Chicago to California.

While some women were beating egg whites, I was beating opponents in court. The last thing I wanted to do when I
dragged myself home at 9 P.M. was slice and dice and tap my
toes until onions glowed translucent.

But something changed when I took a few months off between jobs to regain my equilibrium. In an instinctive move
to take care of myself, I began to cook. I chose easy, homey
recipes, like whole wheat bread from *The Tassajara Bread*

Book, comforted by the miracle of dough rising and the fragrance of loaves in the oven. Long before Whole Foods or Dr. Oz, I was drawn to rainbow chard, Walla Walla onions, purple carrots, and Early Girl tomatoes, produce that popped with color, freshness, and flavor at my local health food store.

Then I went back to work, where litigation chafed against nurture. Time and patience were in short supply. I reverted to takeout food.

But memories of fresh-baked bread and steamy bowls of homemade soup stayed with me, my version of Proust's madeleines. The law firm fed my bank account; my home-cooked meals fed my soul.

Determined not to lose it all, I signed up for a five-day cooking and meditation workshop at Tassajara, a Zen retreat center in the Santa Lucia Mountains near California's Carmel Valley. There I gleaned valuable information: vegetables are sweeter baked than steamed, walnuts less bitter when blanched. But I discovered this wasn't a "how-to-cook" class. It was about paying attention. We tasted stews and salads after adding each ingredient, naming the change with our new lexicon of food: salty, sour, pungent, spicy. Earthy, nutty, bitter, sweet.

During that week, anxious without the busyness of work, I volunteered in Tassajara's kitchen, tearing lettuce for salad. Lined up three to a side at a butcher-block island, our cutting boards cheek to cheek, we sliced the cores off red-leaf lettuce, then tore and tossed the leaves into buckets. The simple task was calming and taught me an important lesson: tear gently.

That's when I learned the secret of cooking. I had to slow down. The very act of being present as I sliced vegetables and seasoned them, then waited for food to cook in its own time, was as nourishing as the dishes themselves.

Eventually, I left the law and began writing full time—

work I love, that slows me down, keeps me present and fully engaged. I shop at the farmers' market, in sync with rhythms of the seasons. In cooking as in life, I need to keep it simple. (My one French cooking class did me in. Start the quenelles a day in advance? *Mon Dieu!*)

As you might guess, my mother is an endless source of material. In a freewrite about Mom and cooking, this is what I wrote:

> She preferred theater, art, and Manhattan eateries to Long Island carpools, whisking, and whirring. Her idea of cooking was broiled lamb chops, Bird's Eye frozen green beans, and Le Sueur baby peas. I didn't fall far from the tree. My culinary skills dead-ended at salad.

Years later, my mother, now widowed and living alone like me, admired my way of eating. "And you look good," she said, bestowing the approval I'd always longed for. I held my breath and waited for her to add, "Though I liked your hair better last year," but the comment didn't come.

"How did you roast those parsnips?" she asked, as she began to cook healthier, more nourishing meals for herself.

And then one day, I received a letter from Long Island, three thousand miles away. In the handwriting I recognized from my childhood, my mother had copied a recipe for Tuscan Bean Soup with fresh kale and cannellini.

Seven ingredients—just my speed. With my Tassajara lettuce training, I was fabulous at washing and tearing kale. I could sauté onions and garlic, add tomatoes, broth, beans, and fresh thyme. In the upper left corner she had scrawled: "Love, Mom." The soup was savory and sweet.

When my sister read this, she told me her own "Mom recipe" story: the day Mom "helped" organize her recipe box.

Last winter, when my eighty-six-year-old mother was visiting me in Milwaukee, we became housebound as the temperatures plummeted into the single digits. Never one to sit idle, Mom suggested we sort and file my recipes, of which I have hundreds—okay, maybe thousands. I love cutting out recipes. I love trying a recipe for the first time and knowing exactly how to improve upon it. I love getting the vegetables from our organic farm share each week during the summer and trying to figure out what to do with them before they rot. Sometimes I even make up recipes in my sleep and execute them in my dreams. I always thought I invented my fabulous Dijon Mustard with Rosemary Marinade for pork chops (brava!) until I went to a friend's house and she was reading the same recipe from a cookbook.

Mom and I sat and sorted for hours at the dining room table, recipes strewn everywhere. I told her how much I loved learning the process of how ingredients go together and I especially loved Mark Bittman's column ("The Minimalist") where he writes about the idea and principle behind the day's recipe before listing the ingredients. He tells you what you can substitute if you don't have an item on hand, what's worked that he's tried and what hasn't. It's like standing next to him in the kitchen.

My mother said, "You have too many recipes. What does a person need with all of these recipes?"

Who is she? Is there a quota I'm not aware of? She just doesn't get it. This is my hobby, my passion, my joy, a way for me to escape from my professional life and another outlet for my creativity. Worse yet, I left the dining room for a little while and came back to find a mountain of newspaper clippings on the floor. She had cut the recipes out of the articles! "No, no, no!" I cried. "I *love* the articles and want to keep them. I just sat here telling you that for the last two hours! Put those scissors down and step away from the recipes!"

She handed over the scissors, barely looking contrite. The next day, as the wind chill hovered around twenty below, my mother suggested that we catalogue my CDs. *Oh boy,* I thought, *another recipe for disaster.*

I love the way this piece about one short scene conveys the personalities of the two characters through their dialogue and my sister's inner thoughts. With just one line ("What does a person need with all of these recipes?"), so much of my mom comes through. The few details about how cold it is outside make the indoor scene more intimate. I can see my mother clipping away, feel my sister's horror when she sees the shreds of articles on the floor. And she comes up with a "kicker"—a punchy line to end her piece. Not every writer is lucky enough to find one, but it's a satisfying ending that leaves us laughing.

EXERCISE

1. Write about a dish your mother or another relative taught you how to prepare.
2. Write a childhood memory about food.

28

Kitchen Aids

F ROM ROLLING PINS to food processors, kitchen utensils
trigger deep memories and stories that tell us far more
than how to use kitchen equipment. Cooking stories invariably tell of relationships. What recipes were passed down in
your family? For whom did you prepare a meal? They detail
time and place. And they revel in the senses.

In class, I offer a basket of kitchen tools as prompts. A rolling pin, cheese grater, vegetable peeler, flour sifter. One student chose a nutmeg grinder and was transported forty years
back to her childhood in Oudenaarde, Belgium, after World
War II. She described the family kitchen at Bergstraat 72,
evoking a time and place unfamiliar to most of us. By writing
about learning how to cook, she communicated the warmth
of her relationship with her mother.

"*Moulin fabriqué en France,*" the little nutmeg grater
proudly announced on its front. It had to be French. Who
else could come up with such a refined tool? The handle
looked like a pair of giant tweezers, holding a square
load-bin for cheese, nutmeg, or any other small edible
you cared to grate. The middle, its mouth, was a moving round drum with perforated teeth, to bite shreds off
the cheese or spice you were sacrificing, and a handle to
slowly turn the tortured little thing. "Get it over with, will
you? Turn faster," the Gruyère yelled at me.

I started playing with *moulin* when I was about ten years old, maybe younger. We used it to finish off the white sauce. With snippets of brown nutmeg, I drew designs on the smooth white surface, watching them disappear in the mysterious depths of the sauce.

"Taste a bit, see if it needs more salt, more nutmeg," Mama instructed.

"A white sauce is nothing really. Here, try it: Let the butter melt, now slowly add the flour and turning, turning, design an eight. Good. Now slowly add milk, turn a bit faster till all is smooth and soft—no lumps, no clots, just a thick ribbon that you keep rewinding. Now add an egg yolk diluted with the juice of half a lemon, pepper, salt. Done. And to round it all off: *un tour du moulin.*"

I can see her twirling her spoon in the smooth surface of the sauce, drawing a figure eight, which she describes with a wonderful image, "a thick ribbon that you keep rewinding." Even in a freewrite, she has detailed the grinder's parts. Words like "tortured" and "sacrifice," which would normally connote pain, are turned on their heads and used playfully as she personifies the poor Gruyère.

In this next one, we get a peek at a mother who prepares fudge in the middle of the night.

I would wake up at 2 A.M. to the smell of chocolate and sugar wafting through the house and knew that if I didn't drag myself out of bed all would be gone in the morning. In the kitchen my mother would be standing over a thick heavy pot stirring bubbling chocolate. She intermittently held up a dripping spoon, letting brown globs slide down into a glass cup of water where she'd test the consistency, rolling balls of chocolate between her fingers. When the fudge was ready she'd scoop and spread the thick lumpy mass into a tin pie pan. We waited a bit for the fudge to cool. By that time a few more of my siblings appeared, each taking pieces, savoring, and leaving for bed. In the morning there were only crumbs in an empty pie pan.

Just reading that paragraph makes me salivate, because the writer awakens so many senses with specific details and images: the smell of chocolate and sugar, the sound of a bubbling pot, the textural image of her mother rolling balls of chocolate between her fingers. I can see, and practically feel, the brown globs sliding down into a cup of water.

I imagine pajama-clad children stealing into the kitchen, watching, waiting, tasting. The writer doesn't say she felt safe and happy in that moment, but I feel it.

In the next example, an author reminisces about a rolling pin her boyfriend's mother gave her. It's a perfect illustration of how writing about an object may quickly shift from describing the object to telling a story.

I'm standing in the kitchen of my New York apartment holding a rolling pin. A beautiful object, its smooth wood tapers at either end. It's not like the old fifties-style rolling pin with handles. My boyfriend's mother gave it to me and I feel the weight of it. It has expectations. It tells me to be nice and sit still. To smile and not get upset. To take any anger I have out on the dough, not on the people it might belong to. But I have no dough. Is this what I'm to do? Make pies? My boyfriend's mother has perfect, somewhat girlish handwriting. She puts little smiley faces as dots and draws little flowers. Her living room is a miniature with frills and flounces. She cooks. She cooks and cooks. I have been indifferent to food all my life, but I begin to understand it when I eat her cooking—homemade waffles fresh out of the old-fashioned waffle iron smothered in butter and real maple syrup. Mashed potatoes smothered in gravy, with sauerkraut, because her mother is German and you always serve it that way. I see that this is what pleases my boyfriend. He loves to go home and eat this cooking. So here I have the rolling pin. She has given me a rolling pin. Is she literally passing the baton?

I turn to look at the far wall. There is my desk, a wooden door over two file cabinets to make it as long as possible and maximize my space. This is where I feel most comfortable. I can do my work and live in structure and order. I turn from the kitchen table with its porcelain top and the butcher-block-topped caddy on wheels, both gifts from his mother. I sit down at my desk and begin my work.

So many senses have come into play and the meaning extends beyond the senses. The writer feels the metaphorical weight of the rolling pin, the unspoken expectations of how she is supposed to behave.

This short piece expresses the writer's interior thoughts and brims with information: her attitude toward her boyfriend's mother, the mother's efforts to infiltrate the writer's life, the boyfriend's relationship with his family, the meaning of food in our lives, and the writer's truth about who she is.

As an editor, I might want to change the repetition of "smothered" to "covered" or "swimming," but the implication of "smothered" is significant in her situation. In freewrites, we want to allow the subconscious to bubble up.

Sometimes our freewrites generate more topics we can

explore. The writer of this piece might choose to "unpack" each element. She could, for example, move from her inner monologue to writing a dinner scene with the boyfriend's family. She could let us see what they look like, add dialogue and reveal her reactions as dish after dish is served. When you write, think about the ways a character can react, such as spoken words, thoughts, or facial expressions expressed or controlled.

It's only fitting that we end this chapter with dessert—even though, as the next writer confesses, the best thing about her high school boyfriend was that he liked to eat dessert first.

Scoop, I'll go with scoop. I'll go with one big scoop of chocolate and another of something that goes with chocolate. Here's the list: coffee, burnt almond, butter pecan, black raspberry, caramel, cherry vanilla, chocolate mint chip, banana, banana nut, peach, mango, and more, much more.

To eat two scoops of ice cream in a beautiful round bowl on a hot summer day is divine. I take a small spoon and eat the ice cream slowly, feeling how cold it is, how bitter it is, how sweet it is, how smooth and voluptuous and fat-gram-forbidden and absolutely wonderful it is, and again, like I said, divine.

The best, and possibly only, good thing about my sophomore-year boyfriend, Stanley, was that on our dates he liked to eat dessert first. So before going to dinner, we would go to Lambert's and get homemade ice cream, because according to Stanley's teachings, if you don't have room later for salad or vegetables, so what? I would get chocolate and something and he would order double pistachio. After a few minutes of silent enjoyment, he would lean across the table, loft a spoonful of pistachio in the direction of my mouth, look straight into my eyes and say, "Here, Boo-Boo, taste this." He asked me to marry him, but I said no. A lifetime of pistachio? I think not.

I enjoy how she travels from sensate details to memories of Stanley, and how flavors say so much. A lifetime of pistachio? Not for this writer. That would be as unacceptable as a lifetime of plain vanilla.

EXERCISE

1. Look around your kitchen and select a cooking implement to use as a prompt. It can be a rolling pin, garlic press, ladle, blender—anything that triggers a story. As you open drawers or inspect the kitchen appliances on your countertop, a memory will likely come to you even before you make your choice and begin to write. In other words, often we choose prompts because we know there is a story there. Our minds are working before our pens start moving. Take the item back to your desk or writing chair and write for ten minutes.

2. In another version of this exercise, which is fun to do with a group, one person prepares a basket of cooking utensils and each person chooses one to write about. Again, take it back to your seat, hold it, look at it, then write whatever story arises. If someone else chooses the item you wanted, you can write about it anyway.

29

Savoring Life, One Bite at a Time

A SINGLE EXPERIENCE can end up as part of more than one freewrite or more than one piece. In an earlier chapter practicing cooking and meditation at Tassajara was an element of my story about learning how to cook, but writing about cooking led me to explore my relationship with my mother. In another writing session, I wrote about my Tassajara cooking experience from a different angle and then polished it as a piece, telescoping in on one particular class at Tassajara and focusing on the day I learned to pay attention to kale.

The kale on our cutting boards was bitter, earthy, grassy, tart. Soon this would be a delicious raw salad, but we had lessons to learn along the way.

In cooking, writing, and life, Edward Espe Brown advises: Take what you have and dream up something tasty to do with it.

Brown, a Zen priest and master chef, helped found Greens restaurant in San Francisco and has authored several cookbooks, including *The Complete Tassajara Cookbook* and *The Tassajara Bread Book*.

On this warm summer day at Tassajara, he passed the plate of kale around after adding each ingredient, one at a time, so that our group of writers could taste and identify the resulting flavors. We were learning the language of food.

"Show up, start anywhere, make mistakes," Brown advised, as he squeezed the leafy greens between his hands with a bit of salt to make the kale juicy and easier to chew.

Then he added honey for "something sweet in all the bites."

"Some prefer sugar," he said, "but honey adds fragrance and florals."

He added the juice of a lemon (tart), garlic and green onion (pungent).

"You might put in parsley," he suggested, with its grassy stem flavor. Or cilantro, with its flowery, fruity, zesty, tangy flavor—"a high element that sings in your palate."

Brown encouraged us to improvise, creating dishes we'd enjoy with the ingredients at hand.

"You can see me in the way I cook," he said, referring to his favorite foods and feisty moods. "Spicy, pungent, sweet, and sour."

Cooking, like writing, can reflect who we are.

EXERCISE

Use these writing prompts:

1. Add a spice or ingredient with a distinctive flavor to a dish and describe the resulting taste. You might try garlic, ginger, honey, cloves, parsley, or lemon. Whatever ingredient you choose, describe how it makes your mouth feel.
2. How does your cooking reflect who you are?

30

The Bounty of the Season

O N THE FIRST ANNIVERSARY of my father's death, I drove to the produce truck that parked on the frontage road of Highway 101 in Mill Valley, California. I thought I was just buying groceries. But when I came home, I prepared a bowl of fresh apples, oranges, pears, and grapes. On my grandmother's oval white china serving plate I arranged fresh ripe vegetables: deep purple Japanese eggplant; fat, red beefsteak and striped Green Zebra tomatoes; a head of garlic; red onion; yellow, green, and orange peppers. I placed them on a table on either side of a vase of fragrant yellow roses.

I didn't interrupt the experience by writing about it in the moment, but soon after I did a freewrite describing the fruits and vegetables so that I would remember the details. I went on to write about my father:

> My father loved to plant things and watch them grow. He planted roses that twined on a split-rail fence, French strawberries tiny as gumdrops, and pears that ripened like big-bottomed ladies. He nurtured his garden, his children. There was no better way for me to connect with him than through this bounty of the season, an altar to his memory.
>
> Throughout his Brooklyn boyhood, Dad had dreamed of creating a garden. He'd worked out a payment plan

with NYU before the days of student loans, become a doctor, married his sweetheart, had three children, and made it to Long Island. On weekends he puttered in the backyard to warbles and waterfalls instead of the El train that had ricocheted past the second-floor window of his childhood bedroom like a wildcat dragging ten thousand tin cans.

In a corner of the garden, under a blue-green pine, Dad had planted a fiberglass tub, its rim camouflaged by deep green leaves of rhododendron and azaleas that blazed fuchsia and crimson in spring. Into the small hillside above the tub, he had sculpted terraces of flagstone, through which he'd threaded a black rubber hose, fashioning a loop that siphoned water up, thanks to a pump he had hidden under floating lily pads. With the flip of a switch, he heard the soothing sound of his handmade waterfall.

My reverie of flowing water was suddenly interrupted. I remembered the urgency I'd felt to get to my father when my mother called with the news. "Your father says it's time to tell you." Her voice was calm. "He has a fast-spreading form of liver cancer. There is no treatment or cure."

I turned back to my writing.

I looked past the bowl of apples and pears on my altar. Through my window, I saw the garden Dad had planted for me two years before, when he and Mom had visited Sausalito. I remembered him slashing through the groundcover vines with the sharp edge of a square shovel, so that I could grow tomatoes. Beyond the garden, on San Francisco Bay, a Chinese junk, with a single red trapezoid sail, crossed the face of Angel Island.

Another memory surfaced that made me smile. I saw myself at three in a tiny red bathing suit, an adult-size white rubber bathing cap flopping down over my ears. I was splayed out in the Atlantic near our Miami hotel, a South Beach haven for working-class Jews before it became a slick Deco scene.

I remembered my father holding me afloat, the large flat palm of his hand under my belly, while I kicked and churned my arms, sputtering, laughing, until finally, a few days later, I triumphed. I could swim!

Today, when I read my writing about my father, I'm surprised how it takes me back and reawakens a deep sense of loss that is no longer part of my daily consciousness. I'm grateful I wrote with enough detail to keep my father's memory alive. Rereading it helps me reexperience the love.

My best writing comes when I relax and allow it, instead of willing it, when I am an instrument for the writing to flow though me. That's how my pieces about my father unfolded.

Think about ways you can open yourself to inspiration. Perhaps by meditating, listening to music, or, like Beethoven, hiking in nature. The composer thought up some of his best ideas when walking through the Vienna Woods.

Writing about the bounty of the season opened the door to reflections on my father that didn't relate precisely to the topic.

The point of this kind of writing is to see where it takes you.

EXERCISE

Sometimes I create a platter of fresh fruits and vegetables—whatever appeals to me and delights my senses—to use as a writing prompt in my workshops. The students choose an item, take it back to their seats, and let the story unfold.

You can do this exercise yourself by placing five fruits or vegetables on a plate. Take one that strikes your fancy and inspires you to describe it or write a story, recollection, or fiction. This exercise is also fun to do with a group. As in the exercise with cooking utensils on page 123, if someone else chooses the item you want, you can write about it anyway. Set the timer for ten minutes and start writing!

31

A Slice of Life

L EMONS AND LIMES are juicy prompts for writing about
the senses.

One afternoon in Petaluma, as the temperature inched toward ninety degrees, my students and I sat on the narrow front porch of the house we'd rented, chairs squeezed into an oval of shade. Each person took a slice of lemon or lime from the plate I passed around. We tasted, sniffed, felt the texture of the zest and juicy nubs within the spokes of membrane. Ready, go! There were a lot of stories about margaritas that day, as perspiration trickled down our backs. Limes, ice, salt, guacamole, and Mexican trysts. A woman from Iran wrote about couscous from her childhood, tangy with preserved lemons.

What immediately came up in my freewrite was a perception of myself. Then I focused on the sensations in my mouth, and finally moved on to a childhood memory.

I am definitely a lime, not a lemon. An exotic flavor not normally wasted on a glass of iced tea. Tangy with a hint of sweetness hidden beneath the biting surface. The writer, critic, observer—lover of irony and wit. Can a lime be sardonic?

I taste and pucker, the insides of my cheeks drawing toward each other. My lips pursed like Leslie Caron's.

I remember the jellied candy slices that we snuck at

Friday night dinner at Grandma Celia's apartment in Brooklyn. Lemon, lime, cherry, orange, coated with course, granulated white sugar. Sophisticated Chuckles. Grandma is sitting on a bridge chair by the open oven, her knees apart like a tough guy, her head wrapped in a white terry towel to absorb her perspiration as she bastes the chicken to its golden finale.

It doesn't matter that I've left the topic of lemons and limes. I've found an important memory, rich in sensory material that evokes feelings about my family. I can use this topic of dinner at Grandma's for another writing session.

When we did this exercise at a writing retreat in Santa Cruz, one person wrote, "A lime is a lemon with attitude." My thoughts exactly.

EXERCISE

Take a slice of lemon or lime. Taste it, smell it, touch it. Write about the sensory experience or the story it prompts.

32

Mindful Eating

PAYING ATTENTION TO how much food we take in—its tastes and textures, chewing sufficiently, and swallowing— helps us be in the present moment and explore the entire sensory experience. As you'll see in the freewrites below, when writing about taste, we often write about touch, texture, sound, and smell.

At a meditation retreat, we had a silent lunch. Our instructions were to put down our utensils after each bite. Chew, swallow. Then pick up our forks or spoons when it was time for the next mouthful. For people living in the speedy lane of life, it was a challenge to slow down, stop shoveling food in. To eat mindfully. One member of the group discovered that she was putting down her fork between bites to play by the rules, but without thinking, she had started eating salad with her hands.

Years later I went on a silent retreat. "No phones, no laptops, no novels or mysteries." Those were the center's guidelines. I did nothing but walk and meditate, do yoga and spiritual reading. I noticed that I was eating less because I didn't need the psychic energy, fueled by food, to deal with the demands of my daily life. Eating in silence, I tasted each bite. Later I wrote:

I taste the sweet red beet, its flesh the consistency of a peach. The cherry tomato pops open in my mouth as my teeth pierce the taut skin, its pulp sweet and acid, laced with seeds. Tofu, the helpless, blank canvas of food, is white and soft as a cliché maiden's thigh, tasting only of the spices applied. One night I paint it with fresh mint and dill, another with soy and ginger. I add celery for contrast and crunch. Pity the poor tofu. Even the celery offers more—chartreuse color, stringy ribs, and a watery sweetness.

Filoli, thirty miles south of San Francisco, is one of the finest remaining country estates of the early twentieth century, boasting the largest heirloom orchard in private hands in the United States. Each fall the estate hosts an apple and pear tasting. One autumn, I wandered from table to table with Charmaine Moyer, a volunteer with a superior sense of taste, assessing our favorites and trying to put words to flavors.

The Early Strawberry apple truly had a strawberry taste. An earthy, slightly musky aftertaste lingered in the back of my throat. Biting through the tart skin of the Lamb Abbey Pearmain, we tasted the intensely sweet, dry flesh, with hints of wine, cinnamon, and nutmeg.

With some pears we found the sweetness comes first; with others the tang or aroma takes the lead. The Magness was creamy, grainy, and aromatic. "A floral perfume goes up into my palate," said Charmaine. She was more specific about the flowery aroma of Des Urbanistes. "The scent of peony bursts on my tongue. Tang follows sweet."

Charmaine had an endless vocabulary to describe the fruit: brisk, buttery, tender. The taste of cucumber or dill. And one pear she obviously didn't favor: "It tastes like chlorine."

Once again, I realized that I knew the tastes and aromas she was describing because I was familiar with the analogies. I had tasted strawberries and cucumbers, inhaled the ethereal sweet fragrance of a peony and the antiseptic smell of chlorine. From our common life experience, we found a language for apples and pears.

Months later, at a writing workshop, I passed a wooden bowl of apple slices. We bit and chewed them mindfully with our eyes closed. The instructions were "Get out of your head and into your tongue. What happens to the apple in your mouth? How many changes can you notice?" We sat and we tasted—not driving, walking, or watching TV, not talking, reading, or checking e-mail. When we'd finished tasting, we wrote words, not sentences. Many of the same words appeared in people's writing, which read more like poems than lists.

Sweet smell
Smooth and slippery
Rose petal taste
Juice of honey
Sound of determination
Teeth marks show the way
Skin to pulp
Divide, divide, divide
Into one

I like the language here, the way the author touches on various senses: "rose petal taste," "sound of determination," "teeth marks show the way." "Divide, divide, divide into one." In the following example I like the directness of "just wet" and the phrase "symphony of chews." I have no idea what a cat in the bushes sounds like, but the simile makes me smile and brings a visual image to mind.

Crisp
And then
Oh sweet
Finality crunch

And just wet
Sounds like
Cat in the bushes
Sweet lips
Ears flooded
With a symphony of chews
Juice trickling down throat
Settles
Mouth still waters
Collects under the tongue
Lips pucker
Swallow
Swallow
Tongue searches for more

In workshops I sometimes pass around bowls of raisins and almonds, and each writer takes a small handful of raisins and a few almonds. They eat them slowly, one at a time, observing taste sensations and textures. The soft, sweet raisins; the hard, nutty almonds.

EXERCISE

1. Eat a slice of apple mindfully. How would you describe the taste and consistency? What is it like to chew and swallow it?
2. Take a small handful of raisins and a few almonds. Eat them slowly and observe the taste sensations and textures.

For both of these exercises, stay in each moment as you taste, then write about your experience, your observations, or a memory that arose.

33

Olio Nuovo

THIS IS A CHAPTER ABOUT taste, but when writing about Italian olive oil, my first thought is of touch, so I must tell you how the oil feels, streaming from a faucet, running through my fingers onto a piece of fresh-baked bread.

I'm traveling with four American chefs, eating our way through Italy. At a communal *frantoio* in Umbria, just over the border from Tuscany, the olives are pressed into a fine elixir. *Olio nuovo*, literarily "new oil," is grassy green-gold, spicy, pungent, fresh, and clean.

A weathered grandpa arrives on his Vespa with a white plastic laundry basket of olives he's harvested from his yard. Another neighbor, with a larger plot, arrives in a pickup truck and tosses his olives into the hopper.

Someone passes us paper cups half filled with oil from the spigot, toasting us to drink it down. *Mamma mia!* Raspy sharp at the back of my throat. But as a finishing oil on salad or fish or for dipping crusty bread, this is the food of the angels.

I shared the oil with friends and asked them to write about their tasting. For each, it was almost a ritual to taste this special oil. One explored it through sight as well as taste, by the light of a full moon. Her piece has been reworked a bit to smooth it out, but even in its original form, the poetic images of nature enhance our experience of her tasting.

The moon was turning full and the days had been frosty, very cold, but clear. What better way to taste rare Italian virgin oil than by the light of the full moon? I carried the slender clear glass bottle outside just as the moon lifted from the top of the trees. Not even eight o'clock and the night was already chilly in anticipation of the midnight frost. I unfastened the lid and sniffed the oil. The subtle fragrance had the same tang and sharpness as the night air. I gently poured a teaspoonful into the large spoon I had with me. Now the moon was pale and large. It looked paper thin, the color of the late winter jonquils I had picked earlier by my front door.

I held the spoon in my mouth, and the oil flowed over my tongue, mouth roof, throat. I was alive to the flavors, vital, fresh, and glowing. Tender and pale, the newest green, the green that appears in winter like jonquils, shocking and ephemeral. And, not to last.

I like the writer's use of light and color, the metaphor of winter jonquils, shocking and ephemeral. Words like "viscous" or "greasy" might have been accurate, but they wouldn't evoke the delicacy that this piece conveys or the shock when nature surprises us and reminds us of what we have forgotten. Tasting the oil in the context of a ritual under a full moon adds a magical quality and tells us this oil is worth paying attention to.

EXERCISE

Pour an inch of any vegetable oil into a cruet or glass. What does it look like? Smell like? Taste like? Is it thick, bitter, grassy, smooth? What does it feel like if you rub it between your thumb and fingertips? What dish would you prepare with this oil?

PART FIVE

Touch

I MAGINE THE CUSH of velvet or the way sandpaper grates. Compare a cashmere sweater with a boiled-wool jacket. Sense a gentle stroke or a violent slap.

Developing awareness and incorporating a sense of touch add another rich layer to writing, making it more evocative. They enable you to communicate emotion, create three-dimensional characters, and help readers feel they're in the scene.

Let your character wince in a collar buttoned tight over his Adam's apple or let us know she feels luscious in a scoop-necked sweater. You'll show us without telling: he was uptight or she felt sexy.

When you write, think about the environments in which you place your characters. Are they walking on carpets of burgundy silk or rough brown jute mats? Is the upholstery taupe chenille or a pale-blue polyester blend?

Let your character run her hand across the splintered edge of a Formica table or caress the fur of her cocker spaniel. These details have emotional content: the house was decrepit; she relaxed in the comfort of her pup.

Think about being blind, having words spelled into your hand, and making the connection between touch and the world of ideas. Touch becomes sight and thought, a means of communication.

The exercises in this section will help you experience different sensations and evoke them in your reader.

34

Hothouse Flower

D O YOUR FINGERS TURN white in the bitter cold while
you scrape the ice off your windshield in the morning?
Or is it so hot and humid that your clothes cling to the small
of your back and dark half moons of perspiration form under
your armpits? Do you take a hot bath to warm up or shower
three times a day to cool down? Our physical responses to
temperature show without telling. Our readers are more likely
to feel like they're with us or our characters in the scene if we
create images of cold, such as scraping ice, or of humid heat,
like a shirt sticking to your skin.

Little did I know, growing up on Long Island, that I am a
hothouse flower, comfortable in a four-degree temperature
range, sixty-eight to seventy-two.

Until I moved to California, I accepted that there were four
seasons—bright green spring; red and golden fall; painfully
cold, gray, and white winter; and enervating summer, which
delighted me when I was young but sent me running from air-
conditioned house to air-conditioned car in later years.

I went to law school in Chicago, not a good choice for a hothouse flower. Nine months of frigid and windy, three months
of sticky and humid, with three weeks of spring sprinkled in.

I see myself on those winter mornings bundled in fleece-
lined boots; a coat so thick I'm like a child in a snowsuit unable to lower my arms, which are stuck in a T position; ski
mittens over gloves; wool hat pulled over my face with eye

and mouth holes, as if I were about to loot a convenience store. My only crime was being so unconscious that I didn't realize how little I enjoyed below-freezing temperatures.

My morning began in the early gray light with the ritual scraping of the windshield. I held the red plastic scraper clumsily in my gloved and mittened hands, my fingers numb and rubbery white, chopping the ice, skimming layers away, until I could see well enough to drive.

If the car wouldn't start, I'd tromp back up to our third-floor walk-up, sometimes forced to step over our neighbor, who was propped up at the top of the stairs against his apartment door, following his night of excess.

After a year of this, I spent a summer recuperating on the islands of Greece, where the only ice was in my lemonade. I reveled in the clear Aegean, clean, dark inky blue, and the fishermen line dancing at a taverna overlooking a rocky beach on Crete, after they'd hauled in the catch of the day.

Then back to Chicago for Winter, Take Two.

The next summer I worked for a Wall Street firm, just two stops from 14th Street in Greenwich Village, where I lived. In the seventies, New York subways were not air-conditioned, so by the time I arrived at the office in my suit, pantyhose, and heels, I felt like I'd already lived through the day, my fillings ringing with the screech of steel on steel.

At the end of three years in Chicago, I announced to my friends: "I'm driving to the end of the Indiana Tollway and flipping a coin. East Coast, West Coast, I don't care. Just get me out of the middle!"

But I remembered the sticky heat of New York, the roaches in my apartment, life in the mines of the Wall Street firm. "I'm moving to San Francisco," I revised my announcement. Temperate enough for a hothouse flower. And that was just the icebreaker for my love affair with the Bay Area.

I hoped my nephew would move from the Midwest to California for college, but "I love winter," he said. Obviously, a new set of genes has been introduced into the family pool. I, too, like snow, when viewed from an Alpine chalet.

Temperature can dramatically affect our feeling for a scene. In *State of Wonder*, Ann Patchett describes the stiflingly hot lost-luggage room at an airport in Brazil:

> The unhappy people who crowded the office of lost luggage pressed against the stacks of unclaimed suitcases and together they raised the temperature in the little room some fifteen degrees beyond the heat in the vast cavern of baggage claim. A small black metal fan sat on the desk and stirred hopelessly at the air in a two-foot radius.

Sometimes I give the prompt "What is your favorite season?" One student turned spring cleaning on its ear by writing about her cleansing rites as fall darkened into winter.

> My favorite season is now, if only I can slow down long enough to enjoy it. The amber, auburn, and ruby leaves float, fall, and skitter by me, palm-sized, with crisp pointed edges like Picasso's painting of Dora Maar with her sharply pointed nails
>
> From this season I get a burst of energy. It sparks the cleaning of cupboards and closets full of loose pants, shoes, and mismatched socks. I dump the mold-rimmed jars of jams, mayonnaise, and ketchup left too long in the refrigerator. An entire summer has passed!
>
> With winter approaching I begin to gather books, pens, and notebooks—time to fill them.

I like the surprise of "fall cleaning" and the colors she names to describe the leaves that "float, fall, and skitter." I resonate with the jagged edges of the leaves in her simile to a Picasso painting, and enjoy her list of things discarded and her insight that winter is a time to turn inward.

Another student praised winter in the next freewrite, revealing her ability to poke fun at herself—a gift for any writer.

I love winter because it fits my stay-at-home-alone instincts.

In spring, my friends are planting and cleaning. When they ask me about my day, I cover up the truth: I got through eight *House Hunters* reruns, read every page of both newspapers, and walked my toy poodle a half block.

In summer, the questions switch to:

"Wasn't it lovely on your patio today?"

"Yes, it looked like it was."

"Did you go out on the water?"

"I enjoyed seeing it from the couch."

Autumn brings poetic statements from friends about ambling through the leaves. I mumble and change the subject.

Then back to winter again, when my beloved lifestyle is back in fashion.

EXERCISE

Use these writing prompts:

1. Write about a time when you were too hot or too cold. Where were you? What were the circumstances? How did you alleviate your discomfort? Was anyone with you? Did the temperature affect them as well?
2. Write about your favorite season.

35

Fashionistas

W E CAN LEARN a lot about people and characters from
the clothes that they wear. Imagine someone who
hates the feel of slick polyester, feels itchy in a lamb's-wool
sweater, or suffocates in spandex. Do you make judgments or
have a visceral response?

What about those who would wear wool for the sake of
fashion on a hot, humid day in Mexico? I was one of these
fashionistas—twenty college juniors and seniors, winners of
Mademoiselle magazine's Guest Editor Competition in 1968.
We would write and edit the August issue, and our trip to
Mexico was part of the package. Even though Mexico City
was sweltering, we boarded the Aeronaves flight in New York
wearing our outfits of brown-and-white-tweed, pleated wool
skirts with matching capes, ivory wool turtlenecks, opaque
brown tights, short brown leather gloves, and brown stacked
heels, because we knew photographers would be there to record our fall fashions as we disembarked.

"Just the ticket for Mexico in June!" my friend quipped.

The next day we sweated and posed in front the Teotihua-
can pyramids, wearing our ensembles, our hair in ponytails,
flips, and pageboy fluffs.

More than forty years later, the guest editors had a re-
union. Some still had their skirts and capes. Even those
who'd let them go remembered them clearly. I sent them an

e-mail asking for their recollections, and they filled in details I'd forgotten, like the leatherette vests.

One added a helpful fashion tip, which hadn't occurred to the rest of us: "The underside of the vest left brown jumblies on my white shirts, so I took clear contact paper (then new on the scene) and lined the inside with cutout pieces. The vest was so stiff it didn't make much difference that I'd added a layer of plastic!"

Another of our group, who went on to design costumes in Hollywood, balked at the "menswear fake leather," and several people recalled that the sweaters itched, a valuable sensory detail.

One of our best archivists (who kept her outfit, though she confessed she "could definitely not fit into it now") e-mailed us a photo, confirming the epaulets and brown leather-covered buttons on our capes. Another claimed we were not permitted to drink liquids until the photo shoot was over, which led to an e-mail debate. The question was finally put to rest by an assertion so confident, it seemed incontrovertible: "They did indeed have iced bottles of Coke just out of reach and off-camera on that friggin' pyramid in Mexico."

You may not remember details, especially if the event happened long ago. Or you may be writing about a time or incident where you weren't present. Talking to others who were there or who know the facts can help you fill in the blanks. Sometimes the very act of writing will help you remember what you forgot. I'm often amazed when I'm doing a freewrite that details like names, addresses, or lines of dialogue suddenly reemerge.

My sister and I have vivid memories of our annual clothes-shopping trips with Mom on the Friday after Thanksgiving, which I memorialized in this freewrite.

In the plate-glass window, the mannequin with the Mary Tyler Moore flip is wearing the same red plaid wool suit as last year. Fashion frozen in time.

My mother loves brightly colored clothes, like Chinese red and royal blue, and favors polyester over silk. ("No dry cleaning. So much more practical.") She also loves a bargain, so we find ourselves on New York's Lower East Side. Where once there were pushcarts, now there are discount stores run by Hasidic Jews.

I prefer muted colors, taupe and grayed-out greens, when I stray from black or bittersweet brown. Silk scarves and cashmere sweaters. Cotton T-shirts, soft as chamois. My standard "uniform" is a top and bottom in matching neutral colors, a quiet backdrop that makes a necklace pop or creates a canvas for a jacket or shawl.

This isn't my kind of store, but I want to be part of the annual ritual, when Mom buys clothes for "the girls," her children, even though we are close to fifty years old.

I will bring the clothes back to California and decide which to keep and which to give to friends, who may look better than I in certain shapes and colors. It is hard to part with anything my mother gives me. Our connections tug through buttons and threads.

For a writing workshop, I asked people to bring a favorite piece of clothing to use as a prompt. Anything that's your favorite has sentiment attached. To my surprise, everyone *wore* their cherished items to the workshop session! One person wrote about breaking free from her mother.

I'm in love with my red sweatshirt, my version of "When I get old, I'm going to wear purple." I didn't wear red because it was so visible, so vibrant that it wouldn't allow me to be unseen. The unspoken rule was "You cannot outshine your mother. She owns center stage and the main spotlight." Red certainly was not the color for a bit player. Last year, I shifted to a star player, shining with my own light.

Another wrote about what her basketball shirt symbolizes to her.

My Stanford women's basketball shirt makes me feel the way I suppose most women feel wearing Gucci shoes and an Armani suit. I feel my best sassy-self. Take that, world; I'm here.

I remember my therapist asking me when, as an unknowingly lesbian adolescent, had I felt truly good in my own body. It certainly wasn't when my hairdresser aunt brought me a new rhinestone necklace to wear with my frilly tulle prom dress. Then all I felt was humiliation and lack of self-confidence. When I felt great I was on the basketball court, dribbling the ball and then passing it like a flash to Sue under the basket or banking a shot from the outside.

People wonder why so many older women attend the Stanford women's basketball games. If they would look closely they would see that a very, very large percentage of their fans are lesbians—there not to ogle but to cheer and celebrate these young women, so skillful and at home in their bodies, running with a freedom we never had.

Describing a character's clothing can reveal a lot about him or her, as well as the narrator's feelings. In this poignant passage, a writer notices her elderly father's outfit:

White cotton socks sagged below his pant legs. A worn leather belt cinched up his baggy khakis, the only one he could buckle by himself now. The holes on the end of it, stretched with use, were tucked into the belt loops of his pants and coursed around to his side. His familiar gray flannel shirt was too big in the shoulders; the cuffs were rolled up at his wrists. When, I wondered, had his shirts outgrown him?

I am particularly touched by the line that this was the only belt he could buckle by himself now.

EXERCISE

Write about the following:

1. Tell me about your favorite piece of clothing, now or in the past.
2. What colors and fabrics do you like to wear? What is your standard "uniform"?
3. Describe the clothing one of your characters is likely to wear. Let the clothing reveal aspects of the person's life and style.

36

Clay Idylls

C LAY IS SENSUAL, like skin," the artist Susan Hall tells
the group of writers and artists who have gathered in her
Point Reyes studio. We've been writing all morning, and now
each of us stands before her own block of brown modeling
clay, eight-inches square, preparing for a hands-on exercise.

Susan espouses the virtues of clay: It is plastic. You can
make mistakes and get rid of them. Above all, she promises,
"Working with clay gets you out of your head."

She suggests that we close our eyes and let our hands explore the clay. She gives us permission to do anything we like
with it.

The experience was visceral, and that's exactly where one
writer went with her freewrite when I gave the prompt "The
Feel of the Clay." She began with four adjectives that described the clay; then her musings went inward, from emotions to inner organs.

Cold, soft, pliable, heavy. My body, my organs, my ear,
my inner cavities, my flesh, my fat, my roundness, my
womanness, my fears, my desires, the inner recesses of
nowhere. It feels smooth, cool. I want to lie down, take
cover, and hide. Look out through the crevasse, lie back,
see the sky. Inward, outward, moseying along, taking
refuge. Don't want to look. I peek. My heart rises with
liking. Don't want to be interrupted. Close eyes. Keep

going, ripples folding over like the folds of my ear. The lips don't talk. What would it be like to put your hand inside your body and feel your liver, kidneys, ovaries, gall bladder, intestines. Sausage. Sausage. Polish sausage. Pat, pat, pat, coil around, lie down in your stomach. What was lunch? Poop de doop. Carrot soup. The clay was beautiful for a moment hanging in my hand then collapsing under its own weight. I wish I could suspend when I let go, see everywhere, under, over, no bottom, no top, all around. Walk away. Let it go.

The squishiness of internal organs came up for others as well. Sometimes a similar thread may run through people's freewrites, a shared worldview that makes us feel connected. On the other hand, each person's freewrite may be so different that our individual quirks of mind become our shared humanity.

You may be torn between thinking "I'm so bizarre, what will people think if I say this?" and "I'm so dull, I have nothing to say." Don't be afraid to go to the places that strike you as weird. It's usually honest and great material—perhaps deep, funny, or sad. You may make some amazing discoveries about yourself, and the act of writing will often help you detach from a situation and see it with new eyes. Remember, you don't have to show your writing to anyone.

As for the idea that your life is boring, the ordinary can become extraordinary through the filter of your pen.

EXERCISE

If you don't have access to modeling clay, you can use Play-Doh or even dough made from flour and water. Feel into the material with your eyes closed. See what tactile sensations come up. What words would you use to describe the feel? Then you can do a freewrite using the prompt "The Feel of the Clay."

Here's an alternative way to write about the experience. Immediately after working with the clay or dough, with your eyes closed, write the words and phrases that come up, not necessarily a narrative. For example: "cold and slimy," "pressure to create," "dirty fingernails." Any of those words or phrases can become the topic of a freewrite.

37

Kiss and Tell

REMEMBER THE FIRST time you rode a bike? Your first car? Your first kiss? The first time you did anything is usually a good topic.

My first-kiss story is about a boy in my fourth-grade class. Our family was moving from Queens to a Long Island suburb in the middle of the school year, and he walked me home across a frost-covered field on a cold winter's day in January. As we approached my apartment, he asked shyly if he could kiss me good-bye. A million years ago, and yet I remember his red-rimmed eyes, his runny nose, his trim little-boy haircut from the fifties.

"Yes." I was surprised, but allowed it, then ran home to tell our housekeeper that a boy had wanted to kiss me.

When I give "The First Kiss" as a topic in writing workshops, many of the freewrites involve slobbers and saliva, like the following excerpt about one writer's first French kiss, when she was in high school.

In the car, when we got to my house, he started kissing me in a way that I had never been kissed. The only time that came close was when another boy had tried kissing me and spit ran down my chin because I didn't know that I was suppose to open my mouth. At least I knew what to do this time, but I didn't like it and when I got into the house I was kind of sick to my stomach.

But the first kiss with a particular person may be sensual and romantic. Here's an excerpt from a writer who went to Africa to study a village performance with deep roots in local culture. Each member of the research team had a local assistant to translate from the native tongue to English and offer whatever help was needed. Salifou was assigned to her.

I had been thinking, I mean feeling, really, I mean fantasizing about Salifou's lips for weeks. He has the most beautiful, sensual, thick lips, which I would secretly watch during interviews as he translated obscure passages to me in English.

What was behind that quiet facade—under his skin inside the calm? During meals I would gaze at him eating fish and spitting, so elegantly and refined, the bones out through his soft, thick, sensual lips. I imagined what it would be like to kiss them, for my thin, white-woman lips to meet his strong, expressive African lips.

I pined at this for days. Imagined with curiosity for weeks. And then, there we were. Alone.

We were in my hotel room. I was sitting on the bed with my legs stretched out in front of me, and the laptop on my lap, and he, in a chair next to the bed. My hard drive was dying and in my last moments of denial that this was happening just as my research in Africa began, I was patiently and shyly waiting for Microsoft Word to save some file, the translations and transcriptions Salifou was helping me with.

I was waiting and probably complaining and waiting. That is when he leaned over to kiss me. I'd been waiting for this moment for what seemed like eons, yet, shy and startled, I pulled away.

My computer gurgled—the action I'd commanded it to do was still processing. Slower still, the death of my hard drive. I, without knowing which direction I should, would, could go, leaned over to him as if to say, "Yes, okay."

And there in that strange hotel room in the finally private space we had, away from bustling village life, our lips met. And it was juicy, beautiful, engulfing, tender, loving, pure, strong. I did not know it would lead to the melting of my heart. Disparate worlds merged. There was a whole world inside Salifou's lips, in his mouth, in the sensual communication of our tongues, that would change me forever. My hard drive died and my heart was being born.

Sometimes our freewrites have natural endings; sometimes they are snippets of scenes. And sometimes they are just the beginning. Salifou moved to the United States to be with the writer and eventually they married. The author is continuing to write this story.

I gave this topic, "The First Kiss," in a workshop for divorcing women, anticipating that many would write cathartically about relationships with their exes. But more than one wrote about their babies. I realized how preconceptions about a topic can stifle imagination. Once again, my students showed me a valuable lesson.

I looked into your eyes,
surprised that perhaps I didn't know you yet.
Would I recognize you in a sea of newborn babies?
You, who would become, I supposed,
the most precious love of my life?
I knew you through my body's holding of you—

This being who kicked, and turned, and squished,
and pushed aside my very insides.
How much more intimate could we be?
and I was so happy to hold you,
to look at you,
with all the relief that you were now, officially,
my very own baby.

You were wet, and red,
with enormous feet for a newborn,
vigorous, so alive, so separate,
even while every cell of your body—
save perhaps one—
was made from my body.

My baby. How I would love you.
Starting with my very first kiss.

EXERCISE
_____

Writing prompt: "The First Kiss."

38

Fabricating Stories

M Y HOME WAS HAVING an identity crisis. California
Japanesque meets the South of France.

Redesigning the house after a fire, I wanted the low roof-
line and long rafter tails of Frank Lloyd Wright and the uncluttered space of Japan with a few exquisite objects, artfully
arranged. Combined with a zesty serving of joie de vivre. Zen
elegance and artistry with the right amount of cush.

The ikats I had brought back from Bali were visually beautiful, but they were a tight flat weave. They didn't say cozy and
comfortable.

Chenille was another story.

On my hunt for fabrics for my home, I collected samples
from San Francisco shops and showrooms. I touched them
with my fingers. I sat on them wearing shorts or skirts so that
the backs of my thighs could respond. Soft and soothing, sharp
and itchy.

Colors were one thing, but touching without looking
brought it to another level, as I explored creating a home that
expressed who I am. And just as the words "cozy and comfortable" tell rather than show, touching the fabrics took me
beyond adjectives to a sensory experience.

As I pulled together the styles I admired—uncluttered
space with a Japanese *tansu* chest, Tibetan carpet, taupe chenille couch, and silk embroidered pillows—I thought I was
combining California, Japan, and the South of France. "None

of the above," said a friend. "You've created your own style."
I'd created Laura's house.

To replicate the sensory fabric experience in a workshop, I
use samples of cloth and ribbon that I get from upholsterers. I
hand out bags that all contain similar items and let the stories
unfold. For example, participants might get a swatch of velvet, a piece of chenille, or a length of grosgrain ribbon.

In one workshop I handed out brown paper grocery bags
with two fabrics in each one. My writing prompt instruction
was "Don't look, just touch." Even though each bag contained
a soft chenille, the writers shied away from the sweet and
bland and focused on the other—either a flat-weave pattern
or one with a harsher nap.

> I am such a visual person that it is hard for me to touch
> something to come up with a narrative—or so I thought.
> I reached into the bag. Both swatches felt like upholstery
> fabric—one soft, with a large, nappy feel, and the other
> stiffer with a patterned texture. What popped into my
> head was if I sat on the stiffer textured one with a bare
> butt, it would leave imprints on me. The other wouldn't.
> Where did that image come from? When I was a little
> child, wearing a short dress, the green prickly couch
> in my childhood living room would leave marks on my
> butt and thighs—or, if I lay down to sleep, on my face.

Another writer, who describes herself as a "potty-mouthed
grandma," wrote:

> Prickly people are a pain in the ass. They are forever un-
> able to compromise, often offended, always holier than
> thou, and easily martyred. They take special care and
> handling and, in my opinion, are not worth the cost. If
> you want more drama in your life, get a prickly friend.
> This is also true if you suffer from low blood pressure,

since their behavior will inevitably increase your anxiety level. For some people, like the ones who prefer spirited horses and some forms of kinky sex, prickly friends might be just the ticket, but not for me.

I can feel the imprint of fabric on the first writer's body. I love that without mincing words, the second leapt from prickly fabric to her perspective on prickly people.

EXERCISE

1. What do the fabrics in your home say about you?
2. Write about the floor coverings in your home or your character's home. Is there wall-to-wall carpeting or hardwood flooring? Are there Oriental carpets, Costco specials, or jute mats?
3. Choose a piece of fabric or furniture that has fabric on it. Anything from an upholstered chair to a bed with a sheet. Close your eyes and describe how it feels to the touch. If there's a story locked in the object, let it come out.
4. This exercise is fun to do with someone else. Before meeting, put fabric or another item in a bag for your partner (nothing sharp or dangerous). Reach into the bag your partner has prepared and feel what's there without looking. Surprising our minds can lead to stories that wouldn't have come if we'd planned or thought too long about what to write. You can do this with a single item or you can place two contrasting items in the bag, such as a sponge and hairbrush. The juxtaposition of textures can jog your creativity.

39

Corporal Punishment

WHEN I WAS FIVE YEARS OLD, my father awakened me from a deep sleep and told me to come into the living room.

In my pale yellow flannel pajamas, I followed him down the hall.

"We thought you should see this," my mother said as she waved me in from her armchair, motioning for me to take a seat on the C-shaped sofa, upholstered dark green flecked with red and gold. I sank into the thick feather cushion and turned my eyes where theirs were fixed.

The fifteen-inch black-and-white television that sat on the baby grand was tuned to *Playhouse 90*. A crippled boy limped across the screen on his crutch, helping his mother in their barn. He sang in a high reedy voice and his mother sang back. Some visitors came who looked like kings in robes and turbans. They sang of secret gifts hidden in the boxes they carried. I have never forgotten the words: "This is my box, this is my box, I never travel without my box. . . ." When they revealed what was inside, I was baffled. What five-year-old Jewish girl knows about frankincense and myrrh?

Sleepy-eyed, I sat through *Amahl and the Night Visitors*, an opera in English by Gian Carlo Menotti. At the end, the boy, Amahl, leaves his mother to go off with the three wise men to follow the star to baby Jesus. This is a good thing, it appeared. But back in my bed I couldn't stop crying.

"What's the matter?" my father asked. I couldn't say. I didn't know. But I couldn't stop. It became hysterical sobbing. My father left me to cry it out. Eventually, he came back and gave me a soft potch on my bum to jolt me out of it. The words we use now—*spank, slap, hit*—have a meaner feel, and somehow I knew he didn't want to hurt me. Still I sobbed. Later, he got me up and had me sit in the reading chair in my parents' room while they slept.

What upset me so much was that Amahl abandoned his mother. Left her alone on the farm with no one to take care of her, no company. What startled me was the spank.

EXERCISE

Choose one of these topics as a writing prompt and tell the story that the word evokes:

- The Spanking.
- The Slap.
- The Hug.
- The Handshake.

40

Sybaritic in Sonoma

I F YOU WANT TO AGE as gracefully as fine wine, try sitting in it. Well, not wine exactly, but a bath of warm water with finely crushed grape extracts from stalks, skin, seeds, and pulp mixed with organic essential oils.

Vinotherapy had come to Sonoma, California, straight from Bordeaux, France, promising to bring back baby-soft skin and fight free radicals, which cause premature aging. "Free radicals make cars rust and turn fruit brown," according to the brochure. My chassis was ready for an overhaul.

While I admire the French for not wasting a thing in the culinary realm, I had misgivings about sitting in vines and pulp and being scrubbed with seeds, perhaps emerging a delicate shade of mauve. But the treatments sounded delicious: Crushed Cabernet Scrub with grape seeds, honey, and organic essential oils; Sauvignon Massage with oils of grape, rosemary, mint, and pine; Hot Merlot Wrap with wine yeast and honey.

Even though my memory and imagination house an endless supply of writing ideas, sometimes I try a new experience because I think it may spark my writing. Vinotherapy intrigued me. A new writing topic and sybaritic experience rolled into one. Divine.

The challenge in writing this way is that I'm both the participant and the reporter, the subject and the witness. While "relaxing" during the treatment, I'm taking mental notes, thinking how I would describe what this feels like.

Lying on the massage table, covered by a soft bath towel, I braced myself for the sting of coarse salt and the prick of sharp grape pips. The massage therapist dipped her hands into a bowl filled with a viscous mixture thick with grape seeds, then gently scrubbed me, soothing strokes, neck to toe, no sting. Nubby, but not rough.

I drifted off dreamy in the sun-filled room, though I was startled when I glanced down at my body. Studded with black grape seeds and bits of salt emulsified in grapeseed oil, I looked like a steak au poivre, peppercorns arranged by Jackson Pollock.

After the scrub, she wrapped my arms and legs in a plastic sheet and suggested I meditate for five minutes. Perspiring, I marinated while she prepared my bath. I tried to achieve inner peace, but mostly I kept thinking that as an entrée, my presentation left something to be desired.

When I looked down at myself during the treatment, I thought, *I look like a baked Virginia ham with cloves arranged by Jackson Pollock.* When I went back over my freewrite, I wanted to carry through the French vinotherapy theme, so I changed ham and cloves to steak au poivre. Because I was inside and outside the experience, I could see myself as a character, which allowed me to poke fun at the not-so-lovely entrée.

Describing a different kind of massage, one of my students wrote about visiting a craniosacral massage therapist, who is gifted at relaxing clients' central nervous systems. I had seen the same therapist, and although I hadn't documented the experience, I remembered feeling as though I was floating an inch above the massage table. I pictured a magician's assistant passing a ring around my body.

It's difficult to describe an ineffable experience, but this writer did a remarkable job.

After our hellos and hugs, I lay down with my face resting on the soft flannel face cradle cover. I can see her toes and smile to myself, elated to be on the massage table.

The room is dimly lit and silent. Any background music—no matter how pleasing—would be a distraction, interfering with the meditative state I will soon enter.

She starts with shiatsu on my back. With her fingers, she gently but firmly contacts the space between each vertebra in my spine, calming me immediately. My breathing expands as I let go of tension that has been gripping me physically and mentally.

I turn over onto my back for craniosacral therapy. She sits on the stool beside the table and gently slides her hands under my sacrum. My sacrum responds, moving slowly downward to be supported. I inhale and exhale slowly, an unspoken affirmation that this treatment has begun. She is still.

My stomach starts to gurgle, speaking its sighs of relief. She holds my sacrum in silence, and feeling safe and honored, my mind ceases its chatter. I feel the muscles and bones in my sacrum descend into a bottomless space of tranquil being, and the boundary of her hand and my sacrum dissolve.

Here I am freed from the pain of multiple sclerosis. My rigid and spastic leg muscles calm down. My head quivers side to side, a message from my body that I've yet to fully appreciate. My nervous system cascades deeper into repose and rest. I remember how it feels to be whole.

As I move into fuller relaxation I feel like I am expanding. I feel as if I am the universe. I am touching in on the vastness of life and being. As if the essence of life can be found in the cerebral spinal fluid. The craniosacral treatment gently contacts this fluid and it is amazing.

There is still no music in the room, but the energy of my body and bones sing beautifully with Allison.

The writer's description is specific, but not cold and technical, warmed by sensory words and phrases like "soft flannel face cradle cover," "breathing," and "silence." Then a surprise: she has multiple sclerosis. Her experience seems all the more calming when she compares it with the normal state of her rigid, spastic leg muscles. Reading, I can feel her calm and wholeness.

EXERCISE

Put a small amount of skin lotion or massage oil in your palm and massage it into the back of your hand. Massage your palms, the backs of your hands, each finger, from the base to the tip. How would you describe the skin on the backs of your hands? Is it different from the palms, the pleated knuckles of your fingers, the area around cuticles? Are some parts of your hands more sensitive than others? Sometimes it helps to close our eyes in order to experience tactile sensations. For this writing exercise, describe the different parts of your hands, using whatever similes arise. If a story comes to mind, write it down. Or try the prompt "Using My Hands."

41

The Bittersweet Hereafter

BEFORE THE FUNERAL service began, my brother, sister, and I went into the chapel to say good-bye to Dad, who lay silent in his casket.

"Did I make a good choice?" my brother asked. He, the child who lived closest to my parents, had had to make the arrangements. The pine box was elegant in its simplicity.

"It's just what Dad would have chosen," I said.

We looked over the lip of the casket, but Dad wasn't there. Instead, we saw a hollow shell of our father in a handsome dark suit, pressed shirt and tie, his skin waxen, pumped up and embalmed.

The idea of writing about a corpse may sound ghoulish or sad, but it can result in beautiful, moving writing. In this somber scene in California's Central Valley, a writer describes her father lying in a smooth wooden coffin.

> He hated wearing a suit, so Fred and I brought his worn khaki trousers and a clean sports shirt to the mortuary, even though the casket would be closed for his graveside service. Alice rubbed thick brown polish onto his Red Wing work shoes and we delivered those for his final journey.
>
> After my mother died, I had visited Dad more often. As I drove down the narrow rural road bordered on both sides by vineyards, I would look for the wooden stake

with its painted white tip that marked our driveway among the leafy rows of vines. Sometimes Dad would hear my car in the driveway, but more often I would see him first, sitting in his swing in the yard.

Dad had built the porch swing when he was sixteen years old, and now it hung by chains from the thick branches of the fruitless mulberry tree. It was made of wood, and the back slats were decorated with curved cutouts and painted a jaunty red, less for decoration than for protection from the weather. His transistor radio hung from the chain, and a nail on the armrest held a flyswatter. The lawn beneath the swing was worn bald with the groove made by his Red Wing work shoes.

From this outdoor living room Dad could read the seasons by the angle of the sun on his vineyard. At the vernal equinox, in March, the westerly sun aligned exactly with the rows of grape vines and cast no shadow. The pruned Muscat stumps were leafless and hunched primordial in even rows. By June, there were bunches of green grapes hanging from the vines, shaded from sunburn by spongy green leaves. Dad loved the summer months the most, when the temperature was over 100 degrees and the sunlight lasted into evening.

When I visited, I sat in my mother's webbed lawn chair beside Dad's outdoor swing. My father never missed a sunset if he could help it. Together we would watch the sun drop into our neighbor's vineyard in the west. If there were clouds, they would flame red for a few moments, then fade again to gray.

"I miss Mother," he would sometimes say to me.

"I do too, Dad," I would answer back, my throat starting to tighten and my eyes stinging with unshed tears. It was important to me that he not see me cry.

"I know you do, pal. Don't worry, we'll wait for you," he assured me.

I can't picture my father walking on golden streets or wearing a pair of waxy wings. For him, I think it is summer solstice and perpetual sunlight is greening the fields. Dad is dressed in his denim workpants, soft from labor and laundering, and he's wearing his sun hat, the straw stained with a halo of sweat.

Her thrifty, down-to-earth father liked comfortable, practical clothes—denim pants, a sun hat stained with sweat, and sturdy work shoes. I can see Alice rubbing them with thick brown polish from a round metal tin. I especially love the sensory image and alliteration of the denim workpants, soft from labor and laundering.

I like the specifics when she describes the swing, in particular the unexpected details of the transistor radio and the flyswatter, which make this swing unique. The fact that her father could read seasons by the angle of the sun deepens my understanding of him as a farmer. The dialogue moves me, especially when he tells his daughter that he and Mother will wait for her in heaven.

Sometimes, when writing about this subject, difficult memories may surface, as in the following piece.

Knotted arthritic fingers rest across his chest. I cuddle under the blanket beside my father's waxen corpse, naked in his deathbed. Lips fold upon his ninety-year-old gum line; closed eyes cave into his skull. My fingers run through his matted gray hair.

Settling my head upon his shoulder, I curl beside the bony coldness.

"Dad, I love you. You meant well and wasted your life," I whisper.

A small tear arises, not enough to fall. Dad died anticipating enlightened perfection as reward for decades of crippling pain.

I remember the last time we cuddled together in bed.

Sunday morning's blue and green comic strips rustled atop the gold, crushed-velvet bedspread while I read Snoopy, B.C., and Li'l Abner's Sunday antics. Dad had put down the *Los Angeles Times* financial section to pull me close. His muscled leg enveloped me. I nestled into his large, hairy body, his sandpaper chin rested upon my forehead. A bulge through his underwear pressed and released against my abdomen. Mom had sent me to Dad's bedroom because she used my room for her daily meditation.

Many people have difficulty processing childhood memories, and sometimes we don't want to do a freewrite for fear of where it will take us. If a subject comes up in your freewrite, it may be time for you to work with it. You may want to consider getting professional help if it feels too big for you to deal with on your own, or you may find that writing about it helps you heal.

This writer had no problem going wherever the writing took her. But if you're wary of opening up a topic, place boundaries around it for your writing practice, so that it doesn't leak into your day. For example, you could decide you're going to write for ten minutes, light a candle when you begin, and blow it out when you finish. Or at the beginning of your writing time say, "I am now going to open up this material." When you've finished, say, "I am now closing this material."

EXERCISE

The following exercises may help you get started writing about the ways death has entered your life.

1. If you've seen a corpse, tell us about it.
2. Describe a funeral service you attended. Was it a friend or family member who died? What happened? What did you see? What did you feel?
3. Do you want to be buried or cremated? Why?

PART SIX

A Symphony of Senses

LIKE A COMPOSER combining instrument parts into a score, writers learn to call on all their senses in a single piece. Harmonies emerge, and the whole exceeds the sum of the parts.

What starts as a freewrite about cooking and taste may unfold into a story that includes the sound of the stove burner hissing and popping, the fragrance of loaves in the oven, and the feel of a wooden spoon as you stir a pot of thick soup.

What starts with lying on your belly next to a stream can turn into a sensory delight of motion, sight, smell, and touch, as in this passage from *The Art of Mending*, by Elizabeth Berg.

> I remember the algae swaying seductively in the greenish water, the quick thrill of a school of minnows swimming past, the grit of dirt against the exposed strip of skin at the top of my yellow pedal pushers. I remember the onion-scented smell of the long grass there, and the way it imprinted a pattern of itself against your skin after you lay in it.

The exercises in this section range from how to locate the reader in time and space to how to experience life with all your senses. They cover character development, dialogue, and enhancing writing with metaphors and similes.

42

Oh My Darlin' Clementine

I DISTRIBUTED SMALL clementines, a cross between an orange and a tangerine, to a group of writers to use as a prompt. "Touch it, smell it, taste it," I suggested, as they passed around the bag of fruit. Bite the skin, chew the juicy segments. Write whatever comes up.

One student kneaded her clementine gently, then broke the skin with her thumbnail and wrote.

> A clementine—it's cool in my hand, feels good to hold, like a stress ball, yet it holds desire, possibility, pleasure. Its color comes alive in this drab, beige room. I wonder about its caloric value, concern about its ability to open me to cravings for sweet things—my mind says that is not a good thing—too many points, too much desire. My eyes take in the lush, green trees after the rain and they are fleshy, as I imagine this clementine may be. Open it, open it, see what's inside. I peel it like a layer of clothing—a pungent tart burst. I don't like oranges, my mind says. What does that mean? It's lovely, complete. It doesn't need me. Why am I struggling so? It's a clementine.

I like the way she compares the spongy citrus to a stress ball, the peel to a layer of clothing. She dives deeper than mere talk of fruit, as her mind thinks of desire and possibility.

The clementine becomes a metaphor for cravings, for people or things that don't need her. Then she has a shift in perspective. After all, it's only a clementine.

I did the exercise along with the group and this is what I wrote:

First the smell: sweet and floral. Then the taste of the rind. My teeth leave marks on the acrid skin. The citrus oil bites my tongue.

My thumbnail strips the skin from the fruit, revealing stringy white membrane, like threads of cotton. I pull off a segment and plop it in my mouth, guessing it will pop and spray when I bite down. The juice explodes in my mouth, sweet, acid, refreshingly wet.

The skin of the membrane is like human skin or rubber. Within the segment are small sacks of luscious. The juice runs down my throat, soothing the crackling cough that has been snapping like a firecracker for two and a half weeks.

These clementines are so small. Three equal one piece of fruit, I think, but I've learned to moderate. One piece of fruit equals one piece of fruit. But such a small piece of fruit. On the spectrum between a grape and a grapefruit, so much closer to a grape.

I used to hate the color orange. I remember going to Mexico with Veronica. It was her favorite color. Bright orange hair, Bakelite bangles and bikinis. I had to get a separate room. I had to go to a separate hotel on a separate beach.

I look back over this freewrite and see what came out. There are sensory images I might work into another piece, especially if I'm writing about a character who eats a tangerine or wears clothes and jewelry that match her fiery hair.

Most important, though, the orange color of the fruit brought me to a story. My father had recently died, and Veronica and I were staying at the hotel where my parents had stayed the previous year. It was painful for me to be there. And my grief was sharpened by the contrast of an ebullient travel companion—an acquaintance, not a close friend—who dressed in bright orange day after day.

EXERCISE

For this exercise, I use citrus fruits because you can peel them without a knife. The act of peeling, the taste and feel of the peel—each adds another element. Choose a fruit that looks good enough to eat—an orange, tangerine, mandarin, clementine, or grapefruit. Feel it, peel it, smell it, taste it. Then write about the experience or any story that comes up.

43

Sentimental Journey

FOR YEARS ONE OF my writing students had avoided the site where her daughter's murdered body had been discovered. Eventually she felt drawn to the place by what she described as "an insistent urging" that she couldn't explain. When she arrived, she instinctively lay down on the very spot, in the position in which the body had been found. She placed dowels where her daughter's hands last lay and a pair of her daughter's small, patent-leather shoes from childhood where her feet had been.

I've read my student's story many times. I can recite the details and am always moved to tears. Yet I was surprised when, at a weekend workshop where I asked participants to bring an object of sentimental value, this writer pulled the patent-leather shoes from her bag. To me, they already had a sacred, iconic meaning, as they did for the author.

I knew of the writer's Catholic upbringing, long ago rejected. This freewrite goes to show how beliefs that no longer seem to serve us can add layers of meaning.

I used to make fun of relics. The nuns had taught us the difference between first-, second-, and third-class relics. First-class meant a fragment of the actual body of the deceased holy person. Usually such items were kept in monasteries, in ornate gold frames that had a window, so if you got close enough you could see a bone fragment.

Second-class relics were items that had belonged to the sainted person, and third-class relics were, I think, objects that had been touched by a first-class relic.

Today, I have a relic: a pair of little patent-leather shoes, which belonged to my daughter when she was five years old. They were her prized possession.

My daughter is gone, but the shoes rest in my underwear drawer. On days when her memory seems distant, I can summon her back into my consciousness by putting my hand in the drawer and feeling one of the shoes.

While my daughter was no saint, I have learned the power of relics to summon the spirit of someone who is gone.

On one level this piece takes us beyond the material plane by comparing the shoes to religious relics. On another level, we are grounded when we understand the power of touch. We can imagine reaching into the drawer, feeling the shoe, and remembering. I haven't had this precise experience, but I am emotionally engaged. This is what we want to do when we put writing out into the world—engage the reader emotionally. Using the senses helps us achieve that.

In this freewrite the writer made no conscious effort to solicit sympathy or empathy. But we feel connected when we read how the ordinary act of reaching into her underwear drawer and touching a precious memento allows her to summon back her child.

Objects of sentimental value inherently carry a story, a memory, an emotion. I wrote about two garnet rings my mother gave me. She picked them up at a secondhand store for a song. They had no intrinsic market value: the stones were marred, the gold bands so thin they might snap. They weren't heirlooms laden with our family stories. But they had meaning to me. They said: There are ways your mother knows you. She appreciates your delicate hands, your love of burnished antique gold, and that you are garnet and amber.

Sometimes an object we keep elicits emotion of another kind. For the sentimental object exercise, this writer chose a drinking straw she'd been using as a bookmark. She kept it to remember how she'd been transformed by her trip to Africa and to remind herself how much we waste in our society.

After I came home from Africa, I became keenly aware of just how much we waste in the U.S. We have things we don't need; we have too many things that we think we need; we don't use, reuse, transform, and reuse again the things we have. When I got off that plane and landed on U.S. soil, everything was questioned as it had been in Guinea—but from transformed eyes.

Take this straw, for example. Every time I found it on my desk while cleaning up the all too many things that I have, I had to remember why I saved it. To remind me, why do we need a straw? What is a straw protecting us from? Putting our lips to a probably not very dirty aluminum can of soda? To make it easier to sip juice or water out of a tall glass filled with ice? A toy? Why do we need this long cylindrical plastic thing—the waste of plastic, the waste of the paper surrounding it. I mean, really, what exactly is a straw's purpose in life? I don't think straws even exist in Guinea, West Africa—just as soap, toilet paper, and paper towels don't exist in public bathrooms. A foreign object, a foreign concept, and a silly useless thing that no one would consider even spending the little money that they do have on, this thing called a straw. I'll have to ask my African boyfriend if he even knows what a straw is.

This is how my eyes got changed in Guinea. Why do our sardine cans have a carton around them? Why do we need so many paper towels to dry our hands? And toilet paper, well—is that even necessary? Who invented a straw? When, why? I would forget and remember, remember and forget.

EXERCISE

Try these writing prompts:

1. Choose an object of sentimental value. Describe it, or let the story behind it unfold.
2. As a variation on this exercise, choose an object you've had on display in your home for more than a year. Why do you keep it in view?

44

Mood Ring

EVEN AT THE AGE OF ten, my nephew had a big heart and a strong writing gene that helped him express what he felt. He was going through a difficult time when his teacher gave him this fill-in-the-blanks poem, which I've since used in workshops. It's a vehicle for expressing feelings with similes and images that relate to the senses. The results can be packed with emotion.

Eli and I filled in the blanks on opposite ends of the emotional spectrum. I chose joy, and he wrote about frustration. Eli's poem is hard to equal. Still, this exercise is a good warm-up for writing from the senses for writers of any age. Take a look at our examples, then try one yourself.

Joy

When I feel joy
It is the color yellow—like a sunflower the size of a
 dinner plate.
I hear bells—like the church tower in San Gimignano
 at dusk.
I taste watermelon—like a sweet crunchy snow cone
 from a sidewalk vendor.
I smell roses—like the ones that climbed the split-rail
 fence in my father's garden.
I see sparkles and twinkles—like the fireworks in Salt

Lake City as we lay on blankets beneath the rockets'
red glare.
I feel expansive—like wave upon wave rolling in to the
shore, an overcoat flung open, a woman on the edge
of possibility.
I want to run and laugh.
But I am writing.

Frustration

When I feel frustrated
It is the color black—like oil flowing through the fields.
I hear arguments—like the President and his
colleagues.
I taste insects—crunchy, disgusting, and gooey.
I smell a skunk—like a camper in the woods.
I see nothing—like an elderly, blind man.
I feel defeated—like countries in a war.
I want to run away and never come back.
But I don't.

EXERCISE

Choose a feeling and complete your own poem.

When I feel [name an emotion] _____

It is the color _____—like _____

I hear _____—like _____

I taste _____—like _____

I smell _____—like _____

I see _____ —like _____

I feel _____ —like _____

I want to _____ and _____

But _____.

45

In the Garden

M Y NEIGHBORS HAVE a garden worthy of Monet. When the weather is good, I bring my writing students over for a freewrite. It can be overwhelming—trellises and archways of sweet climbing roses, Peruvian lilies, lavender, thyme. A fountain with a winged cherub brings sound into the scene.

Students are free to describe the scene or choose one thing to focus on. Alternatively, I offer a more general prompt, such as "I remember a time . . ."

One student sifted through memories and insights about her mother that had previously floated below her conscious thoughts:

"And my new house has a big garden. I'm so excited, because I love gardening," my mother said, as if I would already know that about her.

"You do?" I asked, incredulous, remembering the garden to which nothing was done in fifteen years except for occasional lawn mowing by whatever child could be pressed into service. The azaleas that nearly died every Massachusetts winter, the yellow rosebush that sulked unnoticed until one year it burst forth with a profusion of fragrant blooms, to which my mother said, "I don't like these roses much."

Once I helped her put in some pansies in a little bed

by the driveway, and protected it with a flimsy foot-high white wire fence. That was all.

"I never had much time for it," she continued, ignoring my question. "Plus, with you kids and your friends, I knew things would just get damaged. It wasn't worth the effort."

Slowly, memories sprouted. The time she'd driven to a wood and carefully dug up ferns that now pushed up their curled heads every spring in the shadow of the back of the house. The rocks and little plants that turned a small slope into a rock garden. Now I could see, they hadn't just happened like a force of nature. They'd been cultivated in ways I hadn't observed, much less appreciated, by my mother, from a passion and a creativity within her that I had never noticed.

And all the while my brothers, sisters, and I had been growing up according to some inevitable effortless process, I thought, without much help from her.

Perhaps I was wrong about that, as I was about the ferns, carefully planted in the shelter of the cool rocky cellar walls.

Another writer was having a hard time in her daily life—a debilitating illness, her husband out of work. She felt so good in the garden that she allowed her longings to emerge in her freewrite.

I want this garden. I want to live in this garden. I want. I want. I want. I want. I want. I want. I want beauty. I want sunshine. I want red brick and flagstone. I want pink and silver roses and nasturtiums and dahlias and lilies. I want a row of lettuce and chard and squash and tomatoes. I want views of the bay and the Marin hills and apples and hummingbirds. I want potted plants with trailing lantana. I want to live in this garden and hide in this garden and relish this garden. I want to know how to create such a garden and nurture it and make it grow and keep it growing. I want to stay in this garden for a long time.

In a freewrite about her vegetable garden, a writer who loves to cook chose a different angle: how she chooses her plants.

I choose my garden plants not just for the foods themselves but also for how the plants make me feel.

For some, it's about their energy. My tomato vines cannot be contained, escaping out the sides of their mesh towers, tips crowned with dainty yellow flowers.

I don't like to eat green beans, but I planted Blue Lakes this year because of their beauty, their attitude, and their habit of reaching out and twining upward, their lovely little white flowers, almost orchid-like, hiding among their verdant, heart-shaped leaves.

I love to cook with eggplants but I choose my varieties for their colors and shapes, the Rosa Biancas, small and plump with their pink and white or lavender and white stripes, and large Black Beauties, pendulous and deep purple. Their drowsy lavender flowers will be a perfect counterpoint to the bright red and orange zinnias I have planted in their midst.

Sometimes the seduction is in the flowers. I'm not a big fan of yellow squash, but the flowers I can't do without. They are huge, vibrant orange, and shaped like puffy starfish. Look quickly because by evening they will morph into little flower balls.

I hear the bees doing their work on the flowers and I reflect on how this garden is not just the work of my hands.

I've taken writing groups to the garden at Green Gulch Farm. Only twenty minutes from my home, it's easy for me to visit at every time of year. While we don't have the four seasons in all their glory in the Bay Area, the garden helps me remember: for everything there is a season. For my freewrite, I used the prompt "The garden helps me remember."

Tomorrow it will be November. The roses are almost over. They have bloomed and gone. I cannot bring them back.

The garden makes me remember that I am a part of nature, organic and growing. I need periods of rest to go fallow. Instead of forcing myself to produce, produce, let it spring out of me, lush and spontaneous.

No one commands a tree to grow. Growing is its thing, just as the river flows, knowing where to go.

No one tells the weather how to behave. I take that back. We all tell the weather what we'd like it to do. "Stop raining!" I say. "Stop!" I am powerless over sun or rain.

A student reflected on aging, as she surveyed her garden in autumn:

In fall, I take my garden's pulse and my own, too. The feeling now is less about becoming than about bringing what's already here to full ripeness.

The sunflowers, humble but grand, stand seven feet high, their necks bent over like shepherds' crooks from supporting their huge glorious heads. Their bright yellow petals have dropped off, leaving their huge centers studded with seeds, which look like beige cobblestones spiraling from the center like a galaxy. It is a different beauty than the sunflowers had in their youth.

Goldfinches dart and flutter, then attach themselves to the feeder as if they had Velcro on their feet, some pointing north, some pointing south, and others pointing in every other direction on the compass. Their shirtfronts have faded to a muddy green color, but they seem not at all concerned about the change in their plumage.

I check under the shade cloth for my sweet basil. Ah, perfection—it's better than it has been all summer and reassures me that I, too, may have talents that have not peaked.

As part of a writing retreat, we visited the Australian garden in the arboretum at the University of California–Santa Cruz. The plants were surreal, as if God had dropped acid, whipped out a sketchbook, and said, "How weird can I get? I'll make orange flowers that feel like plastic, bottle brushes large and small, silver plants soft as lamb's ears. Then I'll create this complex sex act where a stamen shoots up laden with pollen and once it's brushed by a bee, it only gets pollinated by another insect on the prowl."

Because the plants were so different from those we're accustomed to, one writer was prompted to write about diversity.

Why is it that we can accept and marvel at diversity in plants, but we get so critical of our fellow human beings?

The bright orange psychedelic stamen-laden flowers . . . Why not the barista with the pierced cheek and purple hair?

The big prickly post-bloom brushy thing . . . Why not the old grumpy man scowling in the diner?

The hummingbird rubbing its head against the center of the bloom so the flower can receive the pollen from the plant across the way . . . Why not the leather boys on Folsom Street? Or, for that matter, the Midwestern cheerleaders bouncing and waving their iridescent pom-poms?

Why not?

Why not?

EXERCISE

Visit a park or a garden. Choose a spot that draws you. You can describe the place as a whole or a particular aspect, such as climbing roses or Japanese maples. If a story or musing surfaces, let it come out and write it as it comes.

46

Victoria's Secret

MORE THAN ONE HUNDRED men in dark suits sit in the meeting room at the Ritz Carlton, listening intently to the projected earnings of Intimate Brands, Inc. They are current and prospective investors, some paunchy, some slick, young, and buff.

Lights off. On the screen, models clad in bras and panties do cartwheels and back flips. "This is our Miracle Bra," Liz Curtis, president and CEO, announces. "It sold out in test stores and our feedback is that the liquid enhancer in each cup does not shift with use, resulting in a continued smooth line through the day."

A few faces in the audience crack into grins.

I pull out my notebook and pen, unable to resist a good scene.

Liz is short and compact, with a round face. She will not be modeling lingerie, but she can attest to the joys of the company's new line of body lotions and fragrances. "Angel Divine won the FiFi last year," she says proudly, "the Fragrance Foundation's top award."

She fills us in on new stores in the works. They'll be more contemporary—"very upscale, with crystal chandeliers." She punches a button on her laptop and the prototype store interior appears, complete with a wall of plastic boobs in bras and three headless torsos without arms or legs, sporting demi-cups and thongs (rear view, of course).

"Now I'd like to show you our latest ad campaign. Video, please."

We all try to look serious as the nearly naked model cavorts in graceful, orgasmic delight, back arch, leg kick, slow and smooth.

The saliva level in the room is rising. Seats are creaking. The temperature is an air-conditioned sixty-six, but men are perspiring. I don't want to look any of them in the eye.

Who would come to this presentation? I wonder. I have come for a day of stock presentations to learn more about the world of finance. In other sessions, I have seen companies project images of water treatment plants and circuit boards. This underwear extravaganza catches me off guard, embarrasses me. As we exit, each member of the audience receives a small white shopping bag with shocking pink tissue, hiding the goodies. What's inside? A thong? Creamy lotion? A condom? When a thousand men enter the ballroom for lunch, one hundred of them are carrying small, white, feminine gift bags with shocking pink tissue poking out.

I wrote the notes for this in the darkened room, while the performance was unfolding. I sensed tension, titillation, and irony. All these straight-faced men in structured suits and ties, watching a show that was mildly pornographic but within the bounds of decency. Later I went back and finished the piece.

EXERCISE

Writing prompts:

1. Write about an embarrassing situation in which you found yourself.
2. Tell us about your underwear.

47

Altars and Rituals

I N MY LIVING ROOM I've created a corner of serenity. A low Japanese tansu chest covered by a black silk obi I purchased in Japan, embroidered with silver clouds and orange blossoms. On the tansu I've placed a live orchid with eight velvety, voluptuous, magenta flowers—a mini-homage to Georgia O'Keeffe. It arches on a slender green stem, bowing toward three tall copper candlesticks, burnished brown from age, yet modern works of art. Above the tansu is a Japanese woodblock print of a blue bamboo grove. While I don't sit in front of this "altar" to meditate, every time I look at it, I feel a sense of peace and beauty.

Many people have altars in their homes, altars of all kinds. Some have family photos displayed on a piano. Some have bowls of colorful rocks from their travels or local hikes. Some have bells or singing bowls. Some have favorite trees or a spot by a stream, which serve as places of sanctuary.

One student did a freewrite about preparing her daily altar with objects on which she can meditate, objects that prompt her writing.

I go outside first thing each morning, cut something growing in our yard and place it on a rimmed white plate, along with a dash of salt to symbolize tears, a pinch of sugar for the sweetness of life, and a pinch of brown rice for the grounding within, which I need to hold all spiritual experience.

The amount of salt, sugar, and brown rice vary according to the burdens I carry each day, and the growing things change with the seasons.

This morning I choose desiccated plants. A dried hellebore flower, its crisp brown petals once lime green, stippled dot ends of a grass gone to seed, a cattail no longer fuzzy but stiff like whiskers. The sugar, rice, and salt blend right in.

The beauty of these browns strikes me especially on this morning at the midpoint of summer, when you'd expect a regal, jewel-toned dahlia or gracefully bowing foxglove. But the North Bay, and even the country, is defying all weather expectations, driving us, forcing us to confront nature's power. Nothing is as it seems anymore. Dry is beautiful in July. Blessed water becomes a curse as drought turns to flood in Texas or Mumbai. Eons' worth of white-blue ice erupts into thundering, crashing icebergs, as polar bears forage through dumpsters to survive.

And yet I see the beauty in the brown, the promise in the seed, the hope and faith in the small piles of sugar, salt, and rice. Placed each morning, a ritual, an acknowledgment, a gift of thanks for it all.

I knew about the objects she collected, but wasn't aware of the salt, sugar, and brown rice, which she used to monitor and reflect her feelings. In this freewrite, she thinks about climate change. In another, she might think about a family member. Freewrites can take us anywhere.

Consider what you'd collect if you were to go outside and

create an altar for your day. Perhaps live elements of nature, such as flowers or grasses. Maybe a dry leaf or bird feather to reflect on the seasons of your life, a hearty weed that has a message, or a twig that appears as a symbol. Perhaps a stone with a rounded shape or one that is sharp and striated will draw you.

We had no altars in our home when I was growing up. But looking back, my mother had a daily ritual. She awoke before the rest of us, had her coffee and read the paper in that quiet time before she had to take the command post and get us off to school. Now a widow, in a childless home, she has a different ritual. Every morning she goes to a local coffee shop for coffee, a toasted bagel, and the *New York Times*. These rituals can be comforting and give structure to a day. Your ritual may seem mundane—awaken, take a cup of coffee back to bed, read, meditate, ring a bell. But it centers you to begin your day.

My family's rituals were of the modern American variety, mostly involving food and shopping—Thanksgiving dinner and our annual shopping trip for clothes. We didn't light Sabbath candles or say grace before meals. But my friend Sandhya's family from India (now in New Jersey) is steeped in ritual, especially her grandmother, Nani, who lives for this kind of thing.

I met Sandhya at a writing workshop in Taos. We were drawn to each other's material, because it was so different from our own. I wrote New York funny with attitude; she wrote lyrically of aunties in silk saris, serving tea and sweets to suitors. Even though we lived on different coasts, Sandhya and I were writing partners for several years, e-mailing pieces to each other and giving feedback by phone.

I still love reading her writing about her family, their culture, and rituals, such as this piece:

In our home, it is a crime to drive a new car without doing a *puja,* a sacred ceremony in which we pray to all our family saints and the appropriate gods for their protection and guidance. So, the day that my sister Anjali brings her metallic blue Honda Civic home, I am not surprised to see a hairy coconut on the kitchen countertop; the coconut is the harbinger of a puja.

In the garage Mom and Nani, my grandmother, stand reverently, waiting for Anjali to set up the Ravi Shankar *Chants* CD. A tray on the hood of the car holds a candle, a brass statue of Ganesha, the elephant-headed remover of obstacles, a photo of our family guru, and one of Papa.

"Should we close the garage?" Mom asks self-consciously.

I nod my head. Our neighbors will think we are odd. Praying to a car, the four of us. Pagans.

Anjali shakes her head firmly. "I want the garage open."

Nani looks at us expectantly. She is wearing her white polyester self-designed *salwar kurta,* her sequin-dotted white slippers, and a white sweatshirt. A chiffon scarf is wrapped around her head and her hands are folded under her belly button. My grandmother is in her element. She lives for ceremonies like these.

I listen as she begins to sing *arati* in her deep, rumbling voice. Our in-house priestess, she waves the flame before the car, transforming it into a sacred object.

Om jai Jagdish hare
Swami jai Jagdish hare
Bhakt jano ke sankat
Das jano ke sankat
Kshan men door kare
Om jai Jagdish hare.

Oh Lord of the Universe,
Mighty Lord of the whole Universe,
All Your devotees' agonies,
All Your devotees' sorrows,
Instantly You banish,
Oh Lord of the Universe.

I close my eyes and pray for smooth travels for my sister. Clear roads and careful drivers around her at all times. Easy-to-find parking spaces and no tickets.

I feel somebody nudging me. It is my turn to hold the plate and wave the flame in a clockwise direction.

As I do, Nani begins a prayer to Ganesha.

Her voice is raspy at times and the words fade in her typical style. But I can see that in her mind, cymbals, temple bells, and a harmonium are accompanying her. She rocks back and forth.

When the last arati ends, Mom hands me the coconut.

"Break it."

When we inaugurated Mom's new car a few months ago, I was the official coconut breaker, banging its hard shell on the concrete step leading into the house. I was surprised when it cracked in half, the sweet water spilling everywhere so that there was nothing left to sprinkle on the car.

"No, I'll pound it too hard, like last time."

Anjali takes the coconut and begins banging it on the step. This coconut is tougher and so it is at least half a dozen strikes before she is able to break it in half. She sprinkles the water onto the windshield and the front of the car.

Nani takes this as her cue to begin chanting her mantras, sacred words or sounds that are believed to have the power to transform and protect one who repeats them.

Today, she chants the mantra for safe journeys.

I ask her to sit in the car next to Anjali. Mom and I get into the backseat, and Anjali puts the key in the ignition and turns on the CD player.

Nani begins to chant a prayer whose words I do not know. Her tune of celebration overpowers Ravi Shankar's "*Om shanti shanti shanti*"and transforms our garage puja into a garage party.

EXERCISE

1. Describe your altar. If you don't have one, what elements would it contain?
2. Collect four or five objects from outdoors and arrange them on a surface to make an altar just for today. Write about why you selected these items and what goes through your mind as you reflect—a ritual of being in the moment.
3. What is your morning ritual? How does it make you feel?

48

Succulence

JUST SAY A WORD LIKE *succulence* and you move to a sensory realm. Whether you're describing plants, food, or people, your subjects are juicy and full of life. Granted, succulent
plants are not the most voluptuous, but their leaves and stems
are rich with liquid, and they bloom in the most surprising
ways.

Hard, inanimate objects, such as glass or marble, are not
succulent. Dry lumber is not succulent, but a tree running
with sap might be. Overstuffed furniture may be voluptuous,
but, except in the case of a waterbed, furniture probably isn't
succulent. Are clouds succulent? Is silk or velvet? Think about
using succulence as a metaphor or simile, combining concepts
in fresh ways to create images that grab our attention. "A rose,
succulent after a summer rain." "A baby's succulent toes."

Few foods are as succulent and sexy as figs. In his poem
"Figs," D. H. Lawrence writes about this "female fruit," which
he tells us "has its secrets." Inside he finds "a glittering, rosy,
moist, honied, heavy-petalled four-petalled flower." A friend
sent me this delectable excerpt about the plump, moist fruit
from her travels in southern Italy:

> And the figs! In Oria, Alla Corta di Hyria's figs with bal-
> samic reduction were so succulent they inspired me to
> a *When Harry Met Sally*–like dining performance. Warm
> sweet fig halves slid into my mouth like oysters; their

soft, furry skin a welcome surprise. Eyes closed, head tilted back, I settled into a moment of gustatory ecstasy, the fig's firm roundness heavy on my tongue, until the sweet-sharp tang of a sugared balsamic reduction filled my mouth and returned me to consciousness.

In a garden planted with succulents I sat with a group of writers. When I gave the prompt "Write about someone who is succulent," there were a few gasps, and one person called out, "Are you *sure*?" I was sure, and every person they wrote about was round and three-dimensional. No flat, cardboard characters with that prompt!

One of the workshop participants likened her longtime partner to the plants around us.

Irene is a succulent. Her light skin is furrowed by wrinkles and she fears her neck resembles a turkey's. But there is another side to succulents and to Irene. They can keep going without much care. They can endure where most would perish, and they are capable of glorious blooming at unexpected times. With prickly spines for their enemies, they store great life within and are treasured by the cognoscenti who have had the pleasure of sharing their lives with them.

Another wrote about a friend:

My gardening buddy and Zen sister Rane is succulent, even though she's muscular and wiry—a little whippet, bursting with energy.

A fat red braid down her back, poking out from her duckbill hat. Her holster with pruning shears, machete.

She moves from plant to plant, clipping, talking.

From her I've learned to be fearless about moving plants, dividing plants. "Here, let's split up these irises"—out comes the shovel, out come the plants, out comes the machete, splitting the roots. Then, voilà. On the other side of the house, a whole new row of irises!

A third wrote about her great-grandson, whom she only knew through photos:

He looks to me like a juicy baby—round and full, sweet smelling with a fresh diaper, big brown eyes. I love infants cuddled in my arms, gazing up with a smile for their great-grandma. By the size of him, he is a champion suckler and his mom a verdant provider.

EXERCISE

Use the following prompts to explore succulence.

1. When you think of succulence, do you think of a food, person, plant, or something else? Tell us what the word brings to mind.
2. Write about someone who is succulent.

PART SEVEN

Motion

W E DESCRIBE GREAT SETTINGS; then the characters move. Their actions and behaviors convey their emotions. Describing physical sensations makes the character's experience more immediate. Their faces express their inner lives.

We can feel the motion outside ourselves—the vibration and rumble of a city or the calm of a pastoral scene. We feel our bodies moving through air or water, languid or agitated, serene or stimulated. When we stand on the deck of a boat, the engine's vibration travels up our legs, forcing us to shift our weight to maintain our balance. Sitting on a moving train, we feel our bodies rock with the rhythm. Wherever we are, if we pay attention, we can feel our breath, our heartbeat, the inner workings of our bodies.

Whether writing narrative nonfiction or fiction, you can use the exercises in this chapter to develop sense awareness and make characters (real or imagined) move in ways that are intriguing, believable, and compelling. These exercises will guide you to write about moving your bodies indoors and out, and suggest activities where you can experience movement.

49

Actions Speak Louder Than Words

I WAS RELUCTANT to see the modern "silent" film *The Artist* for months after it was released, in 2011, because there is virtually no dialogue, nary a clever word. The trailer looked corny. But my mother, who has excellent taste when it comes to books, movies, and theater (in other words, I usually agree with her), insisted that "it should not be missed."

When I finally saw it, I was struck by how instructive a film without words can be. Settings, facial expressions, and physical movement tell us what's important. Granted, in this paean to silent films, actors sometimes mug or exaggerate with a toothy grin or downcast eyes to get their points across. The ingénue is happy; her ivories shine into the camera. The leading man, washed up when talkies take over, sets his reels of silent films on fire. Even his dog communicates through behavior, signaling a policeman to come to his owner's rescue by rolling over and playing dead. When the leading man discovers the ingénue, now a successful star, has secretly bought all his possessions at auction, we see the shame in his eyes, feel it from the circumstance of his discovering a room in her home where his personal effects are shrouded in white sheets.

A pulling motion can say "come"; a push can say "go." Characters can pantomime their meanings, just as I do in foreign countries. To indicate cold, I might shiver; for hunger, I might pretend to spoon food into my mouth.

With "show, don't tell" as our mantra, in workshops I let

people choose from a list of adjectives—say, *nervous, depressed,* and *elated*—and ask them to write a few sentences describing a character who is experiencing one of these states. You can do this as a freewrite, but in fact this exercise calls for a bit of thinking. What mannerisms would convey the feeling?

For *nervous* I might write: "She lined up her bread crumbs on the kitchen table with her knife and crossed her legs, her left heel tapping the floor at sixty beats a minute, her right leg swinging as if she were doing the Charleston."

After each person reads her description aloud, we guess which emotion she chose. We seldom get it wrong. While the writing may include the character's inner thoughts, usually it's the body language, gestures, and actions that express the state of being.

When I offered *elated* as one of the options, a student wrote about her granddaughter:

> As always, she didn't walk the narrow path; she ran it, her three-year-old chubby legs churning up the red-wood needles in the half-light, her head back, blonde hair swinging, her laugh bounding along in front of her, leading her on. Every once in a while she'd toss a glance back at me and cry, "Come on, DeeDee, come on!"

In *The Last Lecture*, Randy Pausch describes the scene where he learns that he has terminal pancreatic cancer. The doctor enters the room and knows that Randy and his wife have seen the CT scans of the tumors. A part of Randy, the scientist, collects facts and quizzes the doctor. Another part stands back and observes, impressed by how well rehearsed the doctor is for this difficult conversation, appearing both heartfelt and spontaneous. Dr. Wolff rocks back in his chair, closing his eyes before answering questions. He leans in to

Randy's wife, his hand on her knee. But Randy notes that the doctor doesn't put his arm around his wife, which might be presumptuous. We are in the scene. The doctor's body language expresses concern without overstepping the line.

Facial expressions, too, convey a character's feelings, often "the very soul of what one says," according to Helen Keller. Instead of saying someone is angry, tell us that her mouth was a tight horizontal. Instead of saying someone is uncertain, tell us how he has teeth marks in his lower lip from gnawing it as he contemplated his next move. Think of what you would miss if, like Keller, you could use only fingertips to discern expressions.

A shake of the head means "no" in our culture, a nod means "yes." But sometimes actions or mannerisms belie what's being said. For example, picture a character shaking his head "no" even as he says "yes."

And we cannot make assumptions as we travel the world. In Greece a shake of the head side to side means "yes," and in India, a head waggle—the head smoothly bobbling ear to shoulder—seems to mean "yes, okay."

EXERCISE

Choose one of the following adjectives: *shy, exuberant, critical.* Write for five minutes describing a character who embodies the quality without naming it.

50

Verbs in Motion

ONE RULE OF STRONG WRITING is to declare war on adverbs. Instead of saying, "He ran quickly across the grass," what verbs could you use that convey speed? Verbs that are livelier and more specific, like *sprint, dash, career, race.* Each one conjures up a different image and engages our attention as readers more fully than "ran quickly."

In this example, a writer describes what it was like living with her alcoholic mother. Through her choice of verbs she tells us her emotional states.

> I didn't want to believe it. Once again, here I was, pacing around the large fourth-floor apartment I shared with my mother, sister, and grandmother, scanning the ground below each window. For years I had feared I might find my mother had jumped from one of these. Her brother had committed suicide. Maybe she would, too.
>
> Now I looked down to see a yellow taxi roll up to the curb, the back door swing open, and my mother stumble out. She crumpled in a heap on the grass as the taxi gunned its engine and sped away. Her flowered sundress, once attractive but no longer, bulged over her bloated body, which exposed her too completely as she lay there, drunk and crying, barebacked, sleeveless, and vulnerable.

Shamed again and angry, I tore down the four flights of stairs, hauled her to her feet, and dragged her into the apartment building, out of sight of neighbors. I yanked the elevator door open, shoved her inside, slammed the gate behind us, and glared at my mother as the elevator rose. A head taller than she was, I stared down at her, watching her cry. Suddenly she threw both arms up around my neck, clinging to me, sobbing. I shrank back even as I hugged her in return. I felt disgusted, repelled, angry, longing to rescue her, and hating her for making me feel that I needed to.

From the verbs we see the author is ready to explode, her tension winding up as she paces, then tears down the stairs, hauls, drags, yanks her mother, slams the door, and glares. Her mother stumbles out, crumples, clings, and sobs. These verbs that describe her mother's actions convey no anger or aggression, just a helpless, pathetic alcoholic.

In the next example, a student writes about her aging father's difficulty moving, using verbs that create strong images by showing instead of telling.

From under his fleece nap blanket, he kicked out his legs toward the side of the bed—scooted and kicked, scooted and kicked—until he leveraged himself to sitting. His thin white hair was a scraggle on the crown of his head where it met the pillow. He sighed. It was a big sigh. Feet on the floor, he sighed again and offered his most common expletive, "Shit," a half-hidden whisper full of consonants. He worked himself to standing and then moved slowly out of his room and down the hall, first one side and then the other bearing his weight as he made sure his feet, in their stiff service, could do what he asked of them. Gone was the energetic stride, pant cuffs flipping outward with his confidence.

He paused at the top of the stairs, gathering himself. Then he started down, holding on to the timber railing. In black felt slippers he padded, one foot first to the step below him then the other meeting it, one step at a time.

EXERCISE

Review one of your freewrites and circle every form of the verb *to be*. If there's room for improvement, see if you can come up with more interesting, specific verbs throughout the piece.

51

Shall We Dance?

YOU CAN TAKE YOURSELF back to a time you'd like to write about by playing songs from the era. Just hearing a few bars of Danny and the Juniors singing "At the Hop" or Johnny Mathis crooning "Chances Are," I am back to those days of dance parties and kissing games in the early sixties, in my friend Janet's basement.

When I play "All I Have to Do Is Dream" by the Everly Brothers, I remember being twelve years old in the Lakeville School gym, attending a social dancing class. Our teachers, Mr. Forbush and Miss Wheeler (Mr. Floorboard and Miss Wheelchair, to us sixth-graders), are swooping across the maplewood floor, demonstrating the foxtrot. They're in what they tell us is perfect Olympic position, her left hand on his shoulder, her right arm crooked at a right angle. His left hand holds her right hand lightly, not graspingly, God forbid. His right hand is centered on her back. The music begins and they glide around the basketball court, demonstrating the dance in 4/4 time.

We're lined up, girls along one wall in our shirtwaist dresses, boys against the other. On signal, the boys run across the gym to ask the girls for a dance.

"Please, oh please, don't leave me against the wall for tiny little Richie," I pray to the gods of dance.

Alas, he has hopped over his competitors and is the

first one to bow from the waist and ask me for this dance.

He is short, perhaps a foot shorter than I, and as we lock at least six inches apart for the first slow dance, his eyes are at the level of my Maidenform bra.

Sometimes in class I play the Righteous Brothers' hit "Ebb Tide" as a freewrite prompt, knowing that for people who were teens in the sixties, this was the sound track of sex. For later generations, it would of course be something different. But other times, I give broader prompts about dance and I get an amazing array of writing, from body motion to the kinds of shoes the writers were wearing.

I walk into the hot muggy dance studio that is tucked away in the corner of an arcade across from a bar. I leave one intensity for another—from the lively streets of a sprawling urban Seville to a studio crowded with handsome, sweating flamenco dancers. As I'm crossing the floor, my fat Gypsy friend, who is teaching the class, yells out something crass and cutting to me. I smile at her refreshingly direct ways, knowing that this is a form of endearment. I approach her rolling, buxom body dressed in a form-fitting sleeveless royal blue top and calf-length black skirt. We kiss on both cheeks in the customary Spanish manner. I smell her pungent Spanish cologne masking her sweat as I take a seat in a beat-up wooden chair next to her. She claps her thick hands and stomps her house slipper–covered foot on the floor, the collection of 22-karat gold chains around her wrists and neck vibrating. In perfect rhythm to the dance steps, she calls out to the class with her vivacious Gypsy grin: *"Tóma—que tóma—que tóma—que tóma tóma tóma tóma tóma*" (Take it!). Kids, cousins, uncles, and other family members run in and out of the studio. It is ninety-nine degrees and there are no windows. The dancers are drenched in sweat; droplets surround their floor space.

The wooden particleboard floor is uneven, torn up, like an old country road marbled with potholes. The dancers' pounding feet have driven holes through the floor. I close my eyes; I feel the vibration of my chair. It is an intense vibration, throbbing. It enters my feet and rises up my legs. My body is pulsating; the rhythm thumps me. I hear thunderous pounding; I see horses running. Metal hammering on wood, the one hundred tiny nails grinding deeper into the soles of the dancers' shoes as they forcefully attack the floor, throwing their body weight into the final turn.

With vivid sensory images, the writer has brought me into the scene. I smell the sweat and cologne. I see the form-fitting royal blue top, the gold chains vibrating. I hear the voice of her fat Gypsy friend, the claps of her thick (what a nice detail!) hands. I feel the kinesthetic vibration, the thunderous pounding of feet, the writer's body pulsating, the metaphor of galloping horses. The surprising image of one hundred tiny nails grinding into the soles of the dancers' shoes as they tear the floor apart.

Certain kinds of music—flamenco, salsa, and drumming, for example—evoke bodily responses, sensual or sexual. But any kind of music can trigger a visceral, emotional response, opening doors to memory and imagination.

The following freewrite is tamer but still carries deep emotion, prompted by a black-and-white snapshot of the writer at five, curtsying.

When you were quite young you curtsied for a living. That was our way. Remember Aunt Fanny's apartment on Riverside Drive when Grandma Katie took you over? Each time you visited, they rolled up the rug. You would do a little ballet—an arabesque or two, a plié, first position, another arabesque, a few twirls—and then you'd curtsy in front of Aunt Fanny and her two daughters, Stella and Nellie, and then Fanny gave you a shiny silver dollar. She was very tiny, with her hair in a sparse bun, and her feet didn't touch the floor. That wasn't the only time you curtsied. You took the art of the curtsy to metaphorical heights for years. If it wasn't a knee you were bending, it was a word, thought, or sentence, but there wasn't always a silver dollar reward. After a while, too many curtsies aren't good for your knees, or for your head. When Aunt Fanny died, you went to Riverside Memorial Chapel, and Katie noticed Fanny's earring was on backward and whispered it to you. Katie curtsied when she had to, but her words made up for it. She taught me how to tip my bowl away when I had soup. That's a kind of curtsy too.

This intimate look into her family gives us a hint of the writer's feelings of pressure to perform, rewarded from the start with a shiny silver dollar. The very names of the relatives evoke an era and ethnicity. (If you know New York, Riverside Memorial Chapel is a giveaway that Aunt Fanny is Jewish, perhaps from the affluent Upper West Side.) Aunt Fanny's earring on backward when she was laid to rest catches my attention—an unexpected detail. I enjoy seeing the writer's mind at work as she leaps from bending her knee for curtsies to bending words, and muses about the payoffs.

EXERCISE

Use the following writing prompts:

1. Learning How to Dance.
2. Play a song from a time you want to write about. What images, thoughts, body sensations, memories, or fantasies arise?

52

Horseplay

S OMETIMES A PIECE COMES out fully formed, like Athena springing forth from Zeus's head. Occasionally, it even happens with a freewrite.

At Miraval, a spa in Arizona, I took part in the "Equine Experience." I knew I wanted to write about it but assumed I'd wait until I got back to California. On my last morning there, relaxed and sitting in the sun, I picked up my pen and the entire story flowed out, the humor, dialogue, and rhythm, with a beginning, middle, and end. I barely had to polish it, though I punched up the humor a bit, and made sure I had a good lead and ending.

In Marin County, home to the hot tub and peacock feather, I thought I knew the alphabet of self-realization, abs to Zen. But I would have to travel to the base of the Santa Catalina Mountains to become enlightened by the Equine Experience.

When the spa specialist described it to me, I laughed.

"Don't laugh." She sounded offended. "It's profound. You learn a lot about yourself."

With a PhD from the Woody Allen School of Obsessive Introspection, I was skeptical. My psyche has been plowed, fertilized, and tilled, and I hoped there wasn't too much more to unearth. But this travel agent, whom I imagined in a warren of cubicles at some isolated outpost with an 800 number, had passion for her horse experience. I was intrigued.

Six months later, I ended up at Miraval, less than an hour from Tucson. My plan was to sleep, do yoga, and get a massage every day. Practicing mindfulness on vacation, once I arrive at mindlessness, I figure I'm there.

As a former lawyer, cross-examining other guests on activities they'd enjoyed to date came as second nature. Workaholic lawyers from New York gave two thumbs down to workshops where they were told to write about their work, then make believe they *were* their work.

"Are you from New York or California?" one asked. "California? You'll like it."

But even the most corporate, Ivy League, untherapized among them touted the Equine Experience.

It sounded simple. First you groom a horse. Then you get it to walk, trot, and canter, using nonverbal cues. Thinking I should do something beyond vegging out, I signed up.

There were just two of us, me and Val, a buoyant real estate broker. Wyatt, the therapist cowboy, would shepherd us through the experience.

We sat on bales of hay and got some basic facts. To the horse, you are a predator. But the horse is more powerful than you are. Horses don't understand words like *Whoa* and *Giddy-up*. They do understand body language. They pick up on threats and fear, and they will react.

Moving into the ring, Wyatt demonstrated how to groom Monsoon, a two-story ton of horse with a ticklish spot. He taught us how to approach the horse and where to touch him to establish rapport.

The first task was to clean Monsoon's hooves. When Wyatt pinched the tendons of Monsoon's foreleg, the horse raised his hoof and dropped it into the cowboy's hand. Sometimes. Wyatt cupped the hoof in his hand and cleaned out the dry, caked mud with a sharp hook. On to the next hoof. Then, lordy lordy, he turned the horse around to get to the other side by placing the side of his rib cage against Monsoon's. Keeping a hand on the horse's back, he walked around Monsoon's rump, never losing contact.

When a horse feels fear, I've been told, it may kick out its hind legs and run. A comforting thought as I imagined sashaying around the beast.

Then Wyatt curried and buffed Monsoon, brushed his face, combed his black forelock, mane, and tail. Piece of cake.

Suddenly Val's elbow was piercing my ribs, her eyes riveted on the vicinity between Monsoon's rear legs.

Wyatt was on top of things. "What do you notice?" he asked. Briefed by yesterday's participants, I went to the head of the class.

"His male organ is extended."

We learned this is a good thing.

"That means he's relaxed," Wyatt commented. *Very* relaxed, I thought. And not Jewish.

Wyatt anticipated our every thought. "Don't worry, he won't urinate on you." Well, almost every thought.

"Okay, choose your horses," he said. "Who wants Monsoon?" Neither of us moved.

"What about Si Si?" he asked, indicating a horse half Monsoon's size, a speckled gray. I paused.

"Maybe you don't feel affinity for either horse," suggested Wyatt.

Yeah, right. I don't feel affinity for a horse named Monsoon who's two stories high, has a ticklish spot you'd better avoid, won't lift his hoof even for the master horseman, and when he's groomed elongates his gelded organ so fully you could use it to measure hectares.

Val volunteered to take Si Si. I was led back to the barn.

I chose a brown gelding, an Arabian beauty, tall, dark, and handsome, reaffirming the wisdom that women are attracted to animals who look like them.

His name was Adieu. Perfect, given my state of relationships.

Time to groom. Now picture this. I'm standing in the middle of the ring, afraid to get near the horse. I'm a successful business owner, a mature executive at the top of my field, and I begin to cry. Fearful Adieu will kick me in the face or pick up his hoof and slam it into my delicate hands.

"What's your fear level on a scale of one to ten?" asked Wyatt.

"Six," I said. Liar, liar.

"What's it about?" Power, authority, the obvious answers. The people who kick you in the face, metaphorically.

"That's good," said Wyatt. "He knows you're afraid; now he doesn't feel threatened. Back up and approach again. With confidence."

I backed up, approached, retreated. Three times: marched forward, touched Monsoon's shoulder, pinched his foreleg, ran away. If a larger group had been watching that day, I might have maintained my composure, kept the armor on. But there was relief in letting a four-legged, non-English speaker trigger a release of fear and stress deeply buried under archaeological layers of business success.

Finally, I got the hoof in my hand. Now I was afraid I was going to hurt the horse. I imagined soft little doggy paws, as I prepared to dig in the sharp hook.

Wyatt took the hoof and dug deep, fast, and hard. *Thwack, whomp.* I stood amazed. "It's as hard as a ram's horn," he told me.

I cleaned two hooves, turned the rump around, cleaned the other two. When Adieu tried to pull his hoof away, Wyatt showed me how to pull it back. Apparently a horse responds to boundaries. What a concept.

Then I curried, buffed, and combed, now totally in love with this beautiful, cooperative horse.

As Wyatt led Adieu to another ring, Val confessed she was jealous that I could cry. Her fear, she allowed, was a nine out of ten.

Adieu was free to run. "When you meet a new horse, observe. Let it run out pent-up energy first," Wyatt advised. A good policy beyond the horse.

He showed us how to move Adieu around the rim of the arena. Standing behind the horse, slightly to the side, Wyatt's body faced the animal's rump. The horse was motionless until Wyatt started to walk. Adieu picked up his pace as Wyatt picked up his, occasionally flicking the whip behind the horse, but not touching him. Through body movement he got the horse to walk, trot, canter, and stop. He showed us how to turn the horse around by repositioning ourselves.

Val did it. I did it. There was a certain thrill, though I was still skeptical, believing that the horse was trained, merely going through his paces. "If you think that, take a breath and pause," said Wyatt. I did. Adieu stopped. "Now make him canter." I sped up my pace and Adieu responded.

I felt powerful, though Wyatt was quick to point out that the horse could pulverize me if he chose to.

Back on the bales of hay, Wyatt described the typical response of corporate types who do this for team building. Some root for their colleagues to succeed. Some hope that they will fail. The most common fear of CEOs is that their covers will be blown. Underlings will see that they are shams, Wizards of Oz who have tricked others into thinking they are competent human beings.

At the spa that night, I soaked in the hot tub with the workaholic lawyers from New York.

"What did you learn?" one asked.

"Horse sense," I replied. Reminders important for work and love. That how you hold and use your body communicates more than words. Pick up on the energy. Boundaries are appreciated. An animal that doesn't speak can express more affection than many humans. When you want to get someone big and powerful turned around, put your rib cage against his and walk slowly around his rump.

My experience of grooming a horse gave me a way to write about lessons I'd learned about myself. I used sensory details to help readers imagine themselves in the ring. I described the "two-story ton of horse" with obvious exaggeration, but the other details were accurate: the thwack of the pick in the hoof that was hard as a ram's horn, my imaginings of soft doggy paws. I paused while editing to think how I could convey the maneuver of turning the horse around, walking slowly around its rump, without too many words. The image gave me the kicker I needed for the ending, as I compared grooming a horse to maneuvering in the corporate world.

Obviously, I am not a horsewoman, but some of my students are passionate about these creatures and transport us with sensory and sensual detail in their writing. In the following excerpt, a writer describes going to the racetrack with her father when she was a child.

I just wanted to be near the horses and smell their smell and see them up close. Finally Dad and I were walking hand in hand to the paddock. One or two were looking out, ears flicking to catch the sounds, or pointed forward, alert and curious. And, oh, what ears. What luminous eyes. What sculpted heads and necks. Each part perfect. Each hair shining. I ached to stroke a muscled neck or feel the oat-sweet scented breath against my cheek or hand. Dad must have known. "I'll take you riding again one day," he said.

The first horse to enter the paddock was a gray, darker across the rump, shading to a very pale gray on the neck and shoulders. I was in love. Then the bay pranced out, nostrils flared, black mane and tail bobbing with each step. I was in love again.

And so it went while my father studied the racing form and figured the odds and checked the record of each jockey. He would look up with the attention of a predator watching its prey, seeing beyond the shining coat right down to the bones and sinews, watching the placement of hooves, gauging the strength of hindquarters and breadth across the chest, but most of all sensing the unseeable, into the presence or absence of spirit on this particular day, into the currents passing between horse and rider.

We reached the rail just as the horses moved in a line onto the track with their lead ponies—stately and slow in the early afternoon sun. Riding silks flashed green, red, pink, gold, white. I counted eleven thoroughbreds in all. With that number there could be an upset, a horse no one had ever heard about could win or some horse that was boxed in on the rail and held back could come from behind in the home stretch.

Now they were led to the starting gates. One horse balked and shied away but was forced into position by three men, two at the rear and one at the head. "Never know what's going to spook some horse," said my dad.

The hush both on the track and in the stands belied the crackling tension, which broke sharply with the clang of the starting bell and the slow-motion opening of the gates and the first lunge as hooves dug into the soft earth. The jockeys bent like benevolent tigers over the horses' necks. For the first furlong, the racers were packed tight like a school of fish—a confusion of hooves, fine-boned legs, and flying manes. Then, in an oddly peaceful moment, the first horse drew forward, pulling others after him as if carried by a current of water. For a moment they seemed to flow like lava or like birds borne on some unseen updraft. The illusion lasted only an instant. The race was on.

I am captivated by the flicking ears and luminous eyes, the sculpted necks and oat-sweet-scented breath. She uses lively verbs—*prance, bob, balk, shy, force*. In the final paragraph, I am caught in the poetry of the race, the exquisite imagery that slows down the motion with precise detail (fine-boned legs, for example), yet keeps it flowing like a school of fish, a current of water.

"Where did the image of jockeys bent like benevolent tigers come from?" I asked.

"It just popped into my head." That's what happens when you let the writing write you.

EXERCISE

Describe an animal in motion. Observe how it moves, how it nuzzles, how it rests. You can do this with a pet at home or with an animal at a zoo, park, farm, racetrack, or anywhere else. Feel free to go beyond description to write about your relationship with the animal, or any story that comes to you.

53

Wrapped Attention

W HEN YOU WRITE about how to do something, you are
forced to describe it in detail, step by step, so that your
reader will visualize and understand.

Before my friend Sandhya's wedding, in India, I found myself dressed in a skintight, rose-silk sari blouse and matching
cotton petticoat, staring down at a piece of silk seven yards
long by four feet wide, strewn across the bed. I was a "sari virgin," so the bride's aunties had agreed to help me dress, but
they were nowhere to be found. How was I supposed to transform this flat rectangle of material into a graceful sari?

I called down to the hotel's reception desk with my SOS.

"Madame, we wear suits," the young woman on duty
proudly informed me.

"What about a housekeeper?"

"Our housekeepers are men. But Ms. Shireen is here. Perhaps she can help."

"Do you have safety pins?" asked Shireen. "We'll be right
up."

While her friend Ritu scoured the desk and nightstand
drawers for a sewing kit with safety pins, Shireen announced,
"I won't do it for you, but I'll teach you how.

"First pull the drawstring of your petticoat *very* tight," she
instructed. "You are going to pleat and tuck the skirt of your
sari into it, so it has to hold."

I sucked in my waist and tied the drawstring so tight that I flashed on Scarlett and Mammy in the corset-cinching scene in *Gone with the Wind.*

"Measure out the *pallu,*" she said, referring to the part of the sari that drapes over a woman's shoulder and hangs down her back. I draped five feet of silk over my left shoulder and twisted my back toward the mirror to check that it fell to a becoming length.

"Throw the material for the pallu across the floor, so you can pleat the section that will hang down the center of the skirt."

Throw it on the floor?

If rule number one for sari draping is "Make sure you have safety pins," rule number two is "Make sure your floor is clean."

I flung the silk toward the hotel room door. Shireen showed me how to create pleats of consistent size by opening my palm, fingers splayed, and working the silk back and forth across my hand until I had formed six pleats that overlapped at one-inch intervals. This six-inch-wide swath of pleats would hang down the front of the skirt in the center.

She wove a safety pin through the back of the pleated section so that it would hold together when tucked into the waist of the petticoat. "Isn't this cheating?" I asked. I felt better when she told me Indian women pinned their pleats as well.

Shireen helped me wrap the rest of the silk around my hips to finish off the skirt, reserving the pallu, which she draped over my left shoulder, securing it with another safety pin to my blouse and bra strap.

I ran to the elevator, descended to the lobby, and caught the minivan to the wedding. I prayed the sari wouldn't disassemble as I climbed the van's steep steps, carefully raising the skirt so as not to trample the work of art we had created.

Entering the reception, I sailed past the receiving line like the *Queen Mary* entering New York harbor. I had entered a maharaja's box of jewels—a sea of saris, bright ruby, emerald, sapphire.

"Look! I'm wearing a sari!" I beamed to the bride's mother, a modern Indian woman who now lives in New Jersey.

"Yes." She looked me over. "Isn't it a pain?"

During my sari-draping lesson before the wedding, while Shireen was instructing me, my mind was recording and shaping a story. When she told me to throw the silk on the floor after measuring out the pallu, I thought of the line "If rule number one for sari draping is 'Make sure you have safety pins,' rule number two is 'Make sure your floor is clean.'"

As soon as Shireen and Ritu left the room, I jotted it down, then ran to catch the minivan.

After the wedding reception, I noted down as much as I could remember about how to wrap a sari, but I doubted I'd ever be able to do it on my own.

Later on my trip, when I was in Kerala, a tropical paradise in South India, I asked the lovely hotel manager if she would show me again, thinking she would be a stunning model. I wanted to memorialize each step with my digital camera, perhaps using one of the photos to illustrate a magazine or newspaper article. The morning of my departure, I heard a gentle rap on my door. A shy and homely young desk clerk had arrived to show me the steps. She modestly rolled up the legs of her trousers, revealing her hairy legs; she would wrap the sari over her street clothes. I had no video recorder on my camera, so we slowly went through each action and I snapped photos.

She began with stiff, awkward poses, but by the end of our session, she moved with grace and confidence, more beautiful than a runway model, more elegant than a gazelle. I treasure my movie of the stills, my digital "flip book" of rapt attention.

Describing even the most ordinary activity in detail is a wonderful way to savor a moment, drop readers into a scene, and communicate feelings by showing rather than telling. As writers, we reveal our characters' emotions by letting them do ordinary things.

In *Angela's Ashes*, Frank McCourt describes how he plans to eat his soft-boiled egg. His joyful anticipation lets us know this is an exciting event in the lives of these impoverished children.

I look at my brother Malachy. Did you hear that? Our own egg of a Sunday morning. Oh, God, I already had plans for my egg. Tap it around the top, gently crack the shell, lift with a spoon, a dab of butter down into the yolk, salt, take my time, a dip of the spoon, scoop, more salt, more butter, into the mouth, oh, God above, if heaven has a taste it must be an egg with butter and salt, and after the egg is there anything in the world lovelier than fresh warm bread and a mug of sweet golden tea?

An "egg scene" from my childhood reveals something about the characters in my family. I was only two at the time, so my memory may be faulty, but it's one of those snapshot scenes that has stayed with me forever: We were sitting at the breakfast table in our Brooklyn apartment, my grandpa Benjie, my mother, and I. Grandpa tapped his raw egg with the back of a teaspoon and peeled a shard of shell from the top. He raised the egg, tilted his head back, and through the small hole, he zupped out the contents. Fascinated, I tried it and made a face. I announced my dislike of the experience. "If you really hated eggs, I wouldn't make you eat them," my mother said. "I hate eggs," I announced. "No you don't," she said.

1. Choose an ordinary activity that you know how to do well and write as if you were teaching someone how to do it, using at least three senses. For example:

   - How to hang a picture
   - How to make a bed
   - How to thread a needle or a sewing machine
   - How to peel an apple with a knife
   - How to prepare breakfast
   - How to fold the laundry
   - How to mow the lawn
   - How to back out of the driveway

2. Think of an activity that is different from ordinary daily tasks and describe it in detail—for example, wrapping a sari, making meringue, piercing your ears.

54

Water, Water Everywhere

IN THE WARM INDOOR POOL, I focused on how it felt to move through the water. *How would I describe the feeling?*

Floating on a Styrofoam noodle, I bicycled, cross-country-skied, did jumping jacks. Squeezed my glutes and abdominals, swept my arms in a figure eight. I didn't stop moving for an hour.

Words drifted through my mind. *Silky, viscous, gelatinous.* *Silky* had the right connotation. Luxurious. Gelatinous, no—cold Jell-O or congealed consommé felt too crude.

A skinny six-year-old boy with black goggles jumped from the side of the pool and sent a spray of needling water points. "Sorry," his father apologized. "Henry, stop splashing."

"We're all here to get wet," an elderly woman in a floppy white bathing cap called back cheerfully. I bicycled to the other end of the pool. A little bit of Henry went a long way.

After an hour I flip-flopped to the steam room and thought about how to describe what I felt. It was hard to breathe in the thick, wet air. Pellets of sweat dripped from my face. My skin prickled in the heat. So many clichés came to mind. "Drops of sweat," "heat that prickles." I challenged my imagination.

I remembered a talk by a guru from India on the benefits of meditation, and I silently recited a mantra. Thinking can interfere with serenity. Coming up with new ways to describe can be work.

Once again I saw that when I relax, fresh images arise and new ideas surface with ease, whether I'm in the steam room or at my computer. For my writing, I need these periods of receptivity, as well as periods of sustained effort. Balance and showing up are the keys.

When I asked a group of writers to describe moving through water, one wrote about bodysurfing in the ocean— quite different from floating in a pool.

Bodysurfing at the ocean's edge. It's what we do. No one teaches this—we just learn by doing. Or maybe it's taught so early, we're babes in arms, too little to remember. But we get it, the rhythm. Light bright, full summer, shade in circles under umbrellas. Sound of hollow crashing waves, pounding sand, the inhaling echo as the undertow drags sand gritty back, sucking at the edges of our feet. Smell of ocean, bits of clinging brown seaweed, Coppertone on my sun-baked skin. Wait for the right moment, the pause between waves—run! Enter the pulse and surge, slip into cold water, find a spot among the others bobbing in the waves. Wave coming—quick decision! Ride it up, slip over the top like a roller coaster. Or dive! Dive! Under the lip of froth, come up just in time to dive again into the green salty brew. Look over shoulder—ride this one, paddle paddle, crash, thrown to the sand, wind knocked out, suit fill with sand, face ground into sharp grain. Jump up, laughing, ready for more.

EXERCISE

Describe the feeling of being in water—a pool, lake, ocean, river, bathtub, or any other source. What is the temperature, the feel of the water on your skin? What's the sensation when you move? What does this remind you of?

55

In a Heartbeat

*L*UB-DUB. *L*UB-DUB. Through a stethoscope I hear the beat. But when I am sitting quietly alone, it is more a feeling than a sound. A steady pulsing in my chest, in and out, in and out, the rhythm of my life.

I am practicing being in my body. It's not always easy for a writer who spends so much time in her head. It's easier to locate my reader in time and space than it is to locate myself.

I stand and notice the weight on my feet. Is there more weight on the left side or right, on the ball or heel, on the inside or outside of the foot? I feel my pelvis, my hips, my knees. I don't *follow* my breath—I *feel* it. Inhale, exhale. I notice a pause at the end of the exhale, before breath and life come back into my body. I feel my arms and legs. Can I feel the shape of my skin? Eyes closed, I hear birds and a neighbor's dog. The sweet scent of lilacs takes me back to my childhood garden. I find my place in time and space.

I'm becoming fluid inside my body.

A friend said to me one day, "The greatest thing you can do for yourself is to get to know yourself." To know where I end and you begin and what's in the space between us.

"Now listen to your heart," she suggested. I felt fear at the thought. What if it was erratic? What would be revealed if I listened to my heart? But I turned inward and listened, to my inner life and breath.

It's amazing how much I can learn about myself if I am still and listen. I use this insight in my classes.

In workshops, after a short meditation, ten minutes or so, the writing always seems to be from a deeper place. I give prompts like "I'll never forget the time . . ." or "What I keep coming back to . . ." and suggest that people write the first thought that comes to them. We write about our obsessions, over and over, until we make peace with them. Here, a writer and longtime meditator explored her yearning for ease.

Oh, the yearning for physical and mental ease. The deep release when I can actually hear the waves, the sounds of the world. When I feel my muscles relax, and my breath flow: so gentle, so helpful. And then the counterpoint: the nagging thoughts, the discontented habits of mind.

If I've been sitting still for hours, sometimes I can actually feel the moment that the discontent arises. Will I ever be able to just relax, fully, with what is, without needing such a radical intervention?

With good writing we connect emotionally with our readers. Call it inspiration (breathing in, being alive). Call it intuition. This is the place I want to write from. This is the heart of the matter.

EXERCISE

Sit quietly for ten minutes. If you have a mantra or meditation practice, feel free to use it. If not, follow your breath, each inhale and exhale. Begin with a deep inhalation and a long exhalation. You might find it easier to focus if you follow each in-breath, counting to ten. At the end of your meditation, do a freewrite using the prompt: "What I keep coming back to . . ."

PART EIGHT

Reworking Your Material

AFTER YOU'VE BEEN doing freewrites for a while, you may want to develop and revise them, polish them for yourself, your friends, and family, or possibly for publication. As a writer, I do both, freewriting without a destination and developing "products" or crafted pieces.

In my freewrites, I let the writing come out. Often an image arises that would not have emerged if I'd sat there thinking, pondering, "working" it. So much of life is about performance and creating a product, that sometimes I want to let go of precision and the exactness of words, the need to name things with specificity. I want to let my mind expand in an all-encompassing way, open to insights beyond words, attuned to the bigger, existential questions—What does this mean? What is the point of being alive? I want to feel whole.

But strong writing is specific, not vague. I learn the names of trees and birds. I name the material a shirt is made of. I tell you if a creaky metal fan barely churns the hot night air. We tell our stories with images and details to help readers see, hear, touch, smell, and taste the scene and to ground them in the experience.

When revising, I'm the editor, not the freewheeling writer. I find it easier to edit a printed draft, although I also edit on the computer. Once I've read the piece through, I can see where it's slow, which words or paragraphs should be deleted because they're repetitious, boring, or not on point, which sections should be reconfigured to create a better flow or enhanced with more images and details.

Images and details convey information and emotion. Instead of saying, "He had cereal for breakfast," tell us what kind. A character who eats Fruit Loops is different from one who eats Kashi Go Lean. If you write that you walked down a path lined with Japanese maples, you create a different feeling than if you tell me you walked through a forest of giant redwoods or on a mountaintop thick with pines. If you simply say you walked among trees, I may fill in the blank, but you are not creating the complete imaginary world that readers want from a writer.

In this section, we'll look at ways to transform your freewrites into more developed pieces.

56

A New Way to Say It

WALKING IS GOOD for my writing. When musing, I walk a twenty-minute mile, not too fast, not too slow—a noodling pace. Often a piece I'm working on rolls around in my mind. I silently play with ideas, and as thoughts gel, I may come up with an opening line, ready to write when I get home to my desk.

Sometimes I think about new ways to say things.

Walking through the woods in Blithedale Canyon after a week of winter rain, it's easy to see how clichés are born. The creeks are swollen, thick with silver water that sprints toward Old Mill Park, where the ghost of the sawmill from one hundred years ago flits among the children's swings.

How would I describe the water? Running, rushing, roaring? All accurate, but overused. I play with the clichés as I walk past the stream, mixing adjectives and nouns to break my logical, linear thought.

Roaring roses, rambling streams
Broken river, swollen dreams

Swollen river, roaring streams
broken roses, rambling dreams

Roaring river, swollen streams
rambling roses, broken dreams

Whooshing, tinkling, willing, thrilling.

A word about clichés. They became clichés for a reason—because they're apt descriptions. If you decide to hone and revise, weed them out—go for fresh images: "wrought-iron fence posts like Zulu spears"; "spring grass as bright as parrots' wings"; "words that slipped like minnows through my tears."

There are many resources to help you find language for sensory description. I've pointed to some in this book. Cookbooks, chefs, and food magazines can show you ways to write about smell and taste. On the Internet, you can search a phrase like "describe wine" and find a list of twenty adjectives. For sound, you could read books on music, and for sight, you could read art books or listen to museum audio guides. Good travel writing is filled with sensory descriptions, because they help us experience the place as the writer did.

If you want to be a good writer, write a lot, read a lot, and listen deeply. Your vocabulary will expand along with your world.

EXERCISE

1. Think of new ways to describe these water scenes:
   - A flowing stream or river
   - Lake water lapping the shore
   - Ocean waves breaking on a beach

2. Take a freewrite or piece you're honing and add a fresh image or unexpected comparison.

57

Composting

I ENCOURAGE YOU to show up consistently for your writing. Sometimes my writing commitment to myself is ten minutes a day; other times it may be an hour, three times a week. It depends on my schedule. That means I sit with pen and paper or in front of my computer for the designated time and see what happens.

But what about times when creativity doesn't flow? Sometimes our freewrites may feel stultified, and sometimes it takes awhile for experience to sift through our consciousness and bring perspective.

I've gone through periods when my writing poured out, rich and lively, and other times when my writing seemed wooden. But even in the dry periods, I showed up. While my material was composting, I kept my writing muscles in shape so I was ready when the material was ready to be written.

I remember the day I walked past the fallow fields at Green Gulch Farm. *What a perfect metaphor for writing,* I thought. Just a few weeks earlier, the fields had been lush with rainbow chard and dinosaur kale, and now I saw nothing more than neatly plowed rows of earth. It reminded me how writing, too, has fallow times. I cannot force creativity to come; I can only show up and be willing.

An artist friend writes similarly about the days she spent sitting in front of a blank canvas, waiting for inspiration.

Nothing came, and still she sat. And then, one day, she picked up her brush and created a work of art.

Another friend, an American gardener who has moved to Italy, reflected on her fallow time. "I am a firm believer that if I don't pull within, way, way in, in the winter, it will be harder to be expansive in the spring."

While this book is dedicated to helping you show up and write, when you're creating a piece, I also encourage you to recharge by letting your field go fallow. Have the courage to do nothing and live for a time in the void, even though you may fear creativity will never come again. It will.

It can be relaxing and freeing. That's how I feel in the water or walking through the woods or going on vacation or a personal retreat. I have no agenda. I trust that from this "in between" place of rest and gestation eventually something will come. In fact, from those times of "nothingness" some of my best writing ideas emerge or thoughts recombine in new ways—the way coffee grounds and grass and paper can become something new, a rich fertilizer that helps the garden flourish.

I find this rest time especially helpful when I'm reworking a piece. I may set the piece aside for a day, a week, a month, or more, then revisit it with fresh eyes. But even when I'm feeling stuck, I keep showing up for my writing time. Eventually the dam breaks and the writing flows again.

EXERCISE

1. What are the ways you rest and restore your creativity?
2. Try this prompt: Sometimes I need to rest.

58

Editing and Polishing

WHEN I WAS WRITING an article about the antiques fair in Arezzo, Italy, initially I wrote down my thoughts in the order they came to me as I stood at my hotel window and watched vendors arrive and set up on the piazza. In Version 1 below, my original draft is in roman type and my comments are in bold italics.

Version 1

Arezzo's Piazza Grande is quiet most mornings, a perfect place to sip an espresso at a sidewalk café. *[This sets the mood, but I want a lead that grabs readers' attention and makes them keep reading.]* But the first weekend of each month *[Not accurate—it's the first Sunday of the month and the preceding Saturday]*, the piazza explodes with antiques and energy. *[I knew I'd change this, but wanted to record the feeling of the fair, which transforms the sleepy piazza into an action zone.]*

From Calabria and Campania, Padova and Pistoia. *[I got the names of the regions and cities from talking to vendors. I liked the alliterations and the sound of this line, but wasn't sure how I would use it.]* On Friday night, small trucks arrive in Arezzo's Piazza Grande and unload a treasure trove of gleaming old dining-room tables, paintings, ceramics, jewelry, copper pots, and Murano glass. You'll find an astounding number *[Too vague; how many is "an astounding number"?]* of pocket-watch faces and sculptures of angels and cherubs of every expression. Most things are "old"—nineteenth and early twentieth century, some older, like a fifteenth-century illustrated hymnal. *[I'm reciting facts, haven't yet shaped this into an engaging piece.]* Some vendors provide antiques at their place of business. *[Again, just a fact.]* A furniture dealer from Padova, for example, had beautiful replicas of seventeenth-century Venetian intaglio dining-room tables for 1,400 euros. He could provide the real thing for 12,000 euros.

I could see bringing home an antique gold ring, but I'm not sure about the dining-room set. *[Here I'm toying with an idea that will become my theme in a later version.]* No problem. Vendors at the fair, as well as the many antique shops in Arezzo, will ship around the world.

[Next comes the nut graph—the who, what, when, and where—essential to a travel piece.] The Arezzo antiques fair, Italy's oldest and largest, takes place the last weekend of every month and draws close to 500 vendors who fill the piazza, spill up the hill *["Spill down" makes more sense than "spill up," so this sentence was changed to "climb up the hill and spill down the side streets" in the final version]* to the cathedral and down side streets to the Chiesa di San Francesco, home to Piero della Francesca's masterwork frescoes, "The Legend of the True Cross."

"It's harder work than it used to be," said Giuglia, from Florence, a vendor for the past sixteen years. "Our items aren't necessary to anyone's survival. With the drop in the dollar and the recession, we've lost our best customers, the Americans and other tourists. Even people from Naples and Rome who used to come are staying local with increased gas prices." *[Initially I included Giuglia's quotes, but travel publications want people to travel, so they shy away from the negative. I cut this quote from the next version.]*

"Besides," she says, gesturing to the Doulton figurines and Sheffield plate she imports from England, "everyone's working. No one wants to dust or polish. A vase, two sprigs, and two rocks—that's how they decorate now. 'Minimalista.'" *[I liked the word minimalista; knew I wanted to include that.]*

Giuglia also sells at the Lucca antiques fair, held on the third weekend each month. Arezzo, unlike Lucca, now permits new items to be sold by artisans, but relegates them to a specific section of the fair. *[This piece is about Arezzo, not Lucca, so I deleted this reference to Lucca. Besides, it could be perceived as a pitch for Lucca, since Lucca only allows antiques, not contemporary crafts.]*

Arezzo is still one of Italy's undiscovered gems. *[Cliché.]* Just forty minutes from Florence on the fast train, it forms a geographic triangle with Siena, but is far less touristy. *[Too much information, and not a punchy ending.]*

In my next version I led with my alliterative line. On one of my morning walks, back home in California, I turned the idea of pocket-watch faces over and over, then the line "gold pocket watches with time on their hands" came to me. Now the wrap-up to the first paragraph had a good rhythm and a clever twist.

In the second paragraph, I added details of light and color.

I attempted to convey the look of the piazza, which isn't flat, but slopes oddly. What does "oddly" mean? I deleted the vague adverb in the next version. The article would run with a photo, worth you know how many words.

Version 2

From Calabria and Campania, Padova and Pistoia, small trucks arrive at Arezzo's Piazza Grande on Friday night and unload a treasure trove of antiques. Gleaming wood dining tables, paintings, ceramics, jewelry, copper pots, and Murano glass. Prayerful angels carved from oak, grinning cherubs and gold pocket watches with time on their hands.

Next day in the bright morning light, buyers and browsers saunter into the sloped cobblestone square, surrounded by buildings, ocher and rose, dating back to the Middle Ages.

I continued with details of items you'll find at the fair. In this version, I expanded the piece into a longer travel article, highlighting sights in Arezzo apart from the fair. Ultimately, I decided to focus just on the fair and put the other sights into an "If You Go" guidebook section that often runs alongside the main article. It includes how to get there, where to stay, and what to see.

The piece was better, but it was still dry. So far I had written it without me in it, which is not as interesting for me as a writer or for my readers. So in the third version, I put myself into the story, on the theory that any piece not starring me is in danger of being boring.

I took the idea from my freewrite about being able to pack a ring, but not a dining table, and I gave myself a quest—a search for a memento from the fair that was artful, affordable,

Italian. The quest gave me a structure. Now I had a story line. I hoped the reader would follow me to see if I was successful in my hunt.

I deleted some of the dry facts and part of Giuglia's quote, and added more sensory details of light and shadow, food and wine. I incorporated more specifics about items sold at the fair and a few "glamour" details—famous sons of Arezzo and the fact that *Life Is Beautiful* was filmed there.

I led with the line about prayerful angels and gold pocket watches with time on their hands. For symmetry (so that each item in my list is preceded by an adjective), I added "terra-cotta" to the description of the cherubs. In the second paragraph I positioned myself looking through my shutters as the vendors arrive. Then I sallied out to reconnoiter, and the hunt began. I show up periodically in the piece with a point of view or an action, but the market is the main charac-ter in the story.

My tie-back ending "Artful, affordable, Italian" is punchier than my original ending and harks back to the beginning of my piece, when I defined my quest. I've underlined some de-tails I added in the version excerpted here, which ultimately ran in the *Los Angeles Times:*

Version 3

Prayerful angels carved from oak, grinning terra-cotta cherubs and gold pocket watches with time on their hands. All are stacked on the cobblestones of Arezzo's Piazza Grande.

Through the shutters of my hotel window, I watch vendors unload a treasure trove of antiques: gleaming wood dining tables, paintings, pottery, jewelry, copper pots and Murano glass. As <u>dusk throws shadows across the square,</u> I go out to reconnoiter, excited by the thrill of the hunt. Tomorrow, when the fair opens, I will buy a memento of my Tuscan travels—something artful, affordable, Italian. And small enough to pack.

The next morning, bright <u>sun warms the sloping piazza</u>, silhouetting Arezzo's <u>turrets, ocher, rose and natural stone, against the royal-blue sky</u>. By 9 A.M., I have joined the locals and tourists in search of rare finds and bargains. The Arezzo antiques fair, Italy's oldest and largest, takes place the weekend that includes the first Sunday of each month, just 40 miles from Florence. With 500 sellers from Calabria to Campania, Padua to Pistoia, merchandise fills the piazza, climbs up the hill to the cathedral and spills down the side streets past the Chiesa di San Francesco, home to Piero della Francesca's masterwork frescoes, "The Legend of the True Cross." The <u>jewel-toned frescoes</u> are reason enough to visit Arezzo.

Most items at the fair are from the 19th and early 20th century, but you can find treasures. A 15th-century illustrated hymnal is not the memento for me, but it's in fine condition, pages intact. A few steps away I admire a beautiful replica of a 17th-century Venetian intaglio dining table with three leaves, for $2,100.

"If you want the real thing, it's $17,000 in my shop in Padua," the owner says. I decline his offer to ship it to me in California.

"Business has slowed," says Giuglia from Florence, a vendor for the last 16 years. Gesturing to the Doulton figurines and Sheffield plate she imports from England, she sighs, "More Italian women are working outside the home. No one wants to dust or polish. A vase, two sprigs and two rocks—that's how they decorate now. 'Minimalista.'"

The slowdown can mean good buys. A couple opening a restaurant scored a dozen slightly beat-up but charming old copper pans for the equivalent of $125.

In the antique shops surrounding the piazza, I found everything my imaginary palazzo required, from carved stone mantlepieces to sparkling chandeliers, but not in my affordable, easy-to-pack category.

Although best known for the antiques fair and the Piero della Francesca frescoes, Arezzo offers an interesting mix of art and architecture—medieval, Gothic and Renaissance. Taking a break from browsing, I sit in the shade of a loggia, designed in 1573 by Giorgio Vasari, spanning one side of the piazza. It's a perfect place to people-watch while enjoying the local, hand-rolled pici pasta with a glass of ruby red Sangiovese, fresh green beans with just-pressed olive oil and an earthy, dark espresso.

Vasari was a native son, as was Renaissance poet Petrarch, who popularized the sonnet form. Their homes are open to the public.

After lunch, I walk to the top of the hill, past antique sewing machines, embroidered linens and musical instruments, to the cathedral, backdrop of a scene in the 1997 Oscar-winning film *Life Is Beautiful.* Best-actor winner Roberto Benigni, who created and starred in the movie, was born nearby and used Arezzo locations throughout the film.

In the cool, dark duomo, I trade shopping for art—Piero della Francesca's fresco of Mary Magdalene and two fine glazed works from the Luca della Robbia workshop. If only I could take these home.

Back in the sun, it seems as though my search might be over. I am drawn to the warm patina of brass wall hooks arrayed on a table. At $10 to $12 each, I buy three. Not antiques, but they look old and lovely and are small enough to pack. Each time I use them, I'll be back in Tuscany for a moment.

Artful, affordable, Italian.

EXERCISE

Take a piece that you're revising and come up with an attention-grabbing lead. Add sensory details to help readers experience what you're writing about.

59

Disrobing in a Public Place

W E DO OUR FREEWRITES without self-censoring, but then we have to decide what we feel comfortable putting out into the world. How much do I want to say about my mother? My thoughts about plastic surgery? My idiosyncrasies and quirks? Do I want to let on that I know what "dropping acid" means?

So when it comes to letting others see our work, we might pull back, edit to the point of comfort. We live in a salacious age, where revealing too much gets media attention. I ask myself these questions: Will what I publish hurt someone I love? Will it embarrass me in years to come? Because, thanks to the Internet, it may be available forever.

If we pull back too far and sanitize what we have written, we can squeeze the juice from our material and present a dry, uninteresting palette. We have to walk the line between exposure and discretion. No need to have open-heart surgery on the sidewalk. But a trickle of blood can humanize us and create a trail for our readers to follow.

EXERCISE

Look over a piece you'd like to put out into the world. Have you struck a balance between self-exposure and discretion that is comfortable for you?

The Sixth Sense

IN THE END, writers have to trust what we might call the sixth sense: intuition—their take on situations and people, the truth of the stories they tell. For me, it's about getting quiet and discerning the feeling of "yes." Coming back to center.

Writing helps us sort things out. We go inward to our deepest source. We soar in the cold, clean air. We write from our experience. We explore our imagination. Inward, outward, we take flight and find our place in the world.

May your writing express the richness of your life and take you home again.

Resources

BOOKS ON WRITING

Some of my favorite books on writing are listed here.

Lynda Barry. *What It Is*. Montreal: Drawn and Quarterly, 2008.

Louise de Salvo. *Writing as a Way of Healing: How Telling Our Stories Transforms Our Lives*. Boston: Beacon Press, 2000.

Natalie Goldberg. *Writing Down the Bones*. Boston: Shambhala, 2005.

Anne Lamott. *Bird by Bird*. New York: Pantheon, 1994.

Phillip Lopate. *The Art of the Personal Essay*. New York: Anchor Books, 1995.

Tristine Rainer. *Your Life as Story*. New York: Tarcher/Putnam, 1997.

Pat Schneider. *Writing Alone and with Others*. New York: Oxford University Press, 2003.

Brenda Ueland. *If You Want to Write*. Thousand Oaks, Calif.: BN Publishing, 2008.

William K. Zinsser. *On Writing Well*. New York: Harper-Perennial, 2006.

BOOKS ON THE SENSES

Diane Ackerman. *A Natural History of the Senses*. New York: Vintage Books, 1990.

Helen Keller. *The Story of My Life*. New York: Doubleday, Page, 1903; reprint, Mineola, N.Y.: Dover Thrift Editions, 1996.

Patrick Süskind. *Perfume*. Trans. John E. Woods. New York: Knopf, 1986; paperback, New York: Vintage International, 2001.

Credits

I AM INDEBTED TO authors of books on writing who came before me. So many books have similar exercises that it's hard to know who invented each one, and at this point I don't always know whether an idea for an exercise was my own or had its genesis in something I read. The following books were especially helpful:

Natalie Goldberg. *Writing Down the Bones*. Boston: Shambhala, 2005. A seminal book on freewriting. (See page 7 for Goldberg's rules for freewriting.)

Tristine Rainer. *Your Life as Story*. New York: Tarcher/Putnam, 1997. This book provides several prompts I have incorporated in *Writing from the Senses*, including a variation on the prompt "What this photo doesn't reveal . . ." Many books suggest drawing a floor plan and using it to prompt stories. Rainer's exercise "Building a Memory House" is adapted here in chapter 6, "Drawing Home," and I've used her exercise "Writing a Reverie" in chapter 7, "Let There Be Light." Rainer was one of the first to write about freewriting, which she called Free Intuitive Writing. Exercises used with permission of the author.

Pat Schneider. *Writing Alone and with Others*. New York: Oxford University Press, 2003. This book has wonderful prompts that influenced some of the prompts in *Writing from the Senses*, including the prompt "In this photo you are . . . ," a description of an ordinary activity on page 231, and the first dialogue

255

exercise on page 77, and a character exercise on page 209 of this volume.

My thanks to the following authors for work that was cited in *Writing from the Senses*:

Elizabeth Berg. *The Art of Mending.* New York: Random House, 2004.

Michael Chabon. *The Amazing Adventures of Kavalier and Clay.* New York: Random House, 2000.

D. H. Lawrence. *Selected Poems.* Revised ed. London: Penguin Books, 1989.

Phillip Lopate. *Getting Personal.* New York: Basic Books, 2003.

Frank McCourt. *Angela's Ashes.* New York: Scribner, 1996.

Ann Patchett. *State of Wonder.* New York: HarperCollins, 2011.

Miriam Phillips. "Becoming the Floor/Breaking the Floor: Experiencing the Kathak-Flamenco Connection." *Ethnomusicology* 57 (3): 398.